MIGHTY

MIGHTY

7 Skills You Need to Move from Pandemic to Progress

BRIAN DODD

FOREWORD BY MIKE LINCH

Xulon Press
2301 Lucien Way #415
Maitland, FL 32751
407.339.4217
www.xulonpress.com

© 2023 by Brian Dodd

All rights reserved solely by the author. The author guarantees all contents are original and do not infringe upon the legal rights of any other person or work. No part of this book may be reproduced in any form without the permission of the author.

Due to the changing nature of the Internet, if there are any web addresses, links, or URLs included in this manuscript, these may have been altered and may no longer be accessible. The views and opinions shared in this book belong solely to the author and do not necessarily reflect those of the publisher. The publisher therefore disclaims responsibility for the views or opinions expressed within the work.

Unless otherwise indicated, Scripture quotations taken from the English Standard Version (ESV). Copyright © 2001 by Crossway, a publishing ministry of Good News Publishers. Used by permission. All rights reserved.

Scripture quotations taken from the King James Version (KJV) – public domain.

Scripture quotations taken from the New American Standard Bible (NASB). Copyright © 1960, 1962, 1963, 1968, 1971, 1972, 1973, 1975, 1977, 1995 by The Lockman Foundation. Used by permission. All rights reserved.

Scripture quotations taken from the Holy Bible, New International Version (NIV). Copyright © 1973, 1978, 1984, 2011 by Biblica, Inc.™. Used by permission. All rights reserved.

Scripture quotations taken from the Holy Bible, New Living Translation (NLT). Copyright ©1996, 2004, 2007 by Tyndale House Foundation. Used by permission of Tyndale House Publishers, Inc.

Paperback ISBN-13: 978-1-6628-6949-5
Ebook ISBN-13: 978-1-6628-6950-1

Brian Dodd's Twenty-Five Leadership Axioms

1. Jesus Christ is the greatest leader who ever lived.
2. The Bible is the greatest leadership book ever written.
3. Excellence becomes average when it's all you have.
4. Never confuse exposure with experience. Never confuse experience with excellence and expertise.
5. The greatest quality a leader can cultivate is personal holiness.
6. Focus on transformation over transaction.
7. Prioritize people over policies and procedures.
8. Never institutionalize or celebrate quitting.
9. You can never have enough leaders.
10. Leadership development is about developing the skills, talents, and abilities to accomplish a task or assignment given to you by God. Leader development is about becoming the type of person who can accomplish a task or assignment given to you by God. They are two completely different skill sets.
11. The most important meeting a leader has each day is his or her personal quiet time with God. Quiet times with God should be the first thing that happens every day because it gives you the framework to put the day's events in proper context rather than reacting to them.
12. Books are easily the greatest return on investment a leader can have.
13. The most insulting thing you can do to another person is be late because you are communicating your time is more valuable than theirs and they should just have to wait for you.

14. Pastors are not communicators. They are preachers who deliver a message from God to a specific group of people at a specific point and time in human history about specific issues in their lives.

15. You cannot have creativity without creation. Messed up hair, skinny jeans, a low v-neck, scarves, and tattoos are not creativity. They are style.

16. Nothing changes a human heart like the Word of God.

17. The only successful leadership model is servant leadership.

18. Your level of expectation determines your level of preparation.

19. A person who can't say, "I'm sorry; please forgive me. I was wrong." doesn't understand grace.

20. You're never more like Jesus as a husband than when you apologize to your wife and take the blame for something you did not do so the relationship can be restored. Because that's what Jesus did on the cross.

21. We all sit down to a banquet of consequences from the decisions we've made.

22. Everyone is interesting because God wants to tell the wonderful story of His Son's love for the world through each and every human life. You just have to take the time to find out what that person's story is.

23. Success is determined by what you do each and every day when no one is watching.

24. The only difference between anger and danger is a "D."

25. If you chase two rabbits, you won't catch either one.

To Doug and Barbara Lilley, the two best in-laws a man could ever have. You are the embodiment of the seven principles found in this book, particularly in the area of faith and putting Jesus Christ first in all you say and do. Thank you for being mighty and guiding our family so well from pandemic to progress.

Praise for Brian Dodd and *Mighty: Seven Skills You Need to Move from Pandemic to Progress*

"Brian Dodd is a unique and inspiring writer. He has a gift of pulling in the reader for meaningful leadership and life change. He is a man of high character and conduct that exemplifies the life of Christ. His blogs are a must-read for every leader. It is said that leaders are readers. *Mighty: Seven Skills You Need to Move from Pandemic to Progress* is a must-read for every sports organization, front office personnel, coach, scout, and business leader in America. If there is only one book you read in 2023, read this one and learn leadership principles that will move you from ordinary to extraordinary!"

Kevin Burrell
Area Scouting Supervisor
Chicago White Sox

"Brian Dodd has done it again, only it's better than ever. Brian continues to produce works of art through his writing. His latest work is *Mighty: Seven Skills You Need to Move from Pandemic to Progress. Mighty* is a must-read for pastors. leaders, and business leaders. Brian has a proven track record for producing work that solves problems, provides empowerment, and adds value to his readers. My plans are to pre-order, and I suggest you do the same."

Pastor Thomas McDaniels
LifeBridge Christian Center

"Brian Dodd has done it again. He has written an insightful book on leadership that is timely and pragmatic. The pandemic was more than an interruption. It was a significant disruption creating the need for leadership to navigate waters like we have never seen before. Brian identifies several key leadership components for courageous leadership in this new era."

Mark Marshall
Assistant Executive Director
Georgia Baptist Mission Board

"My friend, Brian Dodd, has done it again! Brian is an unbelievable leader and marries this trait into his writing flawlessly. I have heard Brian speak on the topic of this book several times, and it has moved me to action at each opportunity. I am convinced that this resource will move you into your next step as well. I cannot recommend enough this book, *Mighty: Seven Skills You Need to Move from Pandemic to Progress* or Brian himself. I know you will be challenged and encouraged."

Chad Aukland
Vice President of Consulting
INJOY Stewardship Solutions

"Brian's vision, passion, and tireless efforts to grow those in leadership positions is second to none. Whether you are in the board room or locker room, his words will help you create an environment of teamwork and growth that will propel your business or team to the next level."

Don Baker
Director of Athletics
Cobb County (Georgia) Schools

"Delivered in classic insightful Brian Dodd style in his new book, *Mighty: Seven Skills You Need to Move from Pandemic to Progress,* Brian draws seven essential skills from captivating stories that are critical for great leadership. This book will be helpful to you and those you lead."

Dan Reiland
Executive Pastor
12Stone Church

"Brian is extremely gifted in evaluating the attributes of successful leadership. In *Mighty: Seven Skills You Need to Move from Pandemic to Progress,* Brian does it again with practical applications of those traits, from King David to modern combat veterans. *Mighty,* just like *Timeless: 10 Enduring Practices of Apex Leaders,* is a must-read for any leader as

Brian translates the greatest leadership examples in history into useful lessons to implement personally and immediately."

Jeff Wright
Founder of Wright Wealth LLC
President of US Army Ranger Association

"Brian Dodd has an amazing gift to highlight leadership lessons from things that we all experience in everyday life. His gift of insight, observation, and application are once again on display in *Mighty: Seven Skills You Need to Move from Pandemic to Progress*. We have all been impacted by the pandemic these last few years. A question many have wrestled with is how do we move on or forward from it? Using real-life stories from the Bible and present-day people, Brian shows us the skills we need to move from pandemic to progress!"

Nate Galloway
Discipleship Pastor
West Ridge Church

"Over the last two decades, Brian Dodd has been a consistent voice, encouraging local church leaders to be all God has called them to be and giving them the tools needed to pursue that calling. As we leave the shadow of the pandemic, we emerge into a new season of church leadership, requiring different skills and abilities than were needed pre-2020. Brian's vantage point as a student of the church has equipped him like no other to help us guide our churches into this new landscape, and I am grateful for this gift to the local church."

Matt Steen
Co-Founder
Chemistry Staffing

"As the world continues to recover from the horrors of the COVID virus, I am thankful for individuals (like Brian Dodd), who have the skills and tenacity to evaluate the tragedy and give solutions to overcome. Thanks, BD, for prayerfully discovering the truths of Bible stories that apply to real-life issues that have changed life forever, for many people. In *Mighty: Seven Skills You Need to Move From Pandemic to Progress*, read and listen carefully to your conscience for answers to your life's challenges, to become *mighty*."

Marty Benton
President
Vision Street Ministries

Table of Contents

Foreword xvii

Introduction xix

Chapter 1—Production 1
    Elite Training 2
    Tom Mullins 2
    Jiro Ono 4
    Rafael Nadal 6
    Bryce Young 7
    Zach Wilson 8
    Dak Prescott 10
    Nepalese Sherpa Kami Rita 13
    AquaDom 15
    Breathtaking Health 16
    The Brooklyn Nets 18
    Paul O'Neill, CEO of Alcoa 19
    Highly Efficient 23
    Kansas City Chiefs 25
    Super Bowl LVI 26

Chapter 2—Passion 33
    Nehemiah 38
    Sebastian Steudtner 40
    Andrew Wiggins 41
    Dillon Helbig 43
    Coach Prime, Deion Sanders 45

Chris Paul	46
When the Moment Is Too Big	47
The Grand Tetons	49
Florence Chadwick	52
Bob Salem	54
Zach Wilson	56

Chapter 3—Resilience 63
Two Types of Storms	66
Great Questions	67
Stetson Bennett IV	69
Antarctica	71
Tsunami Survivor Lisala Folau	73
Real Madrid	75
Coach Trent Dilfer	77
Jayson Tatum	78
Coach Kara Lawson	80
Coach Nick Saban	83
Coach Gareth Southgate	86
Steph Curry and P.J. O'Brien	88

Chapter 4—Teamwork 93
Georgia Bulldogs	96
San Francisco 49ers	98
Andrew Wiggins	101
Invasive Species	103
Toxic Bosses	105
The Role, Duty, and Expectation of a Coach	107
Sandcastles	109
Kylian Mbappe	110
World Cup 2022	112
Uriah the Hittite	120

Chapter 5—Contentment 125
The Shaun Wright-Phillips Syndrome	129
Coach Bruce Arians	131

    Coach Larry Brown 132
    Will Smith and the Slap Heard Around the World 134
    Coach Bill Self 138
    Coach Jurgen Klopp 140
    Walter Orthmann 142
    Bees Are Actually Fish 143
    Jurassic Park 145
    Coach Nick Saban 146

Chapter 6—Courage 153
    Ukrainian President Volodymyr Zelensky. 157
    Ukrainian Parliament member Kira Rudik. 159
    Bear Attacks 160
    Darren Harrison 163
    Nick Bostic 166
    Pastor Todd Korasick 168
    Hard Conversations 170
    Seattle Seahawks. 172
    Animal Rain 175
    Jordan Spieth 176
    Big E's Broken Neck. 178

Chapter 7—Faith 183
    Premarital Questions 184
    Movie Night 186
    The Father of the Bride 187
    Highly Effective Fathers 192
    Growing Churches During the Pandemic 195
    Growing Churches Post-Pandemic. 197
    Leader Development versus Leadership Development. 199
    Elite Preachers 202
    Pastor Kevin Lloyd 206
    Pastor Matthew Cornett. 208
    Christmas 211
    Clint Hurdle 211

Conclusion 217
    Kobe Bryant 218
    Who Are the Leaders Worth Following? .220

Bibliography 225

Foreword

If you were to ask anyone what makes people great, or even better, what makes them standout, I feel confident you would get a myriad of answers. Greatness is subjective, but it is always recognized when it is seen. The person exhibiting those characteristics always stands out from the crowd and lives differently than others choose to! They are the difference makers who change every environment they are in or they encounter. They may be school teachers, business owners, coaches, lawyers, doctors, or homemakers, but they have something that is different about them!

My good friend Brian Dodd in his newest book, *Mighty: Seven Skills You Need to Move from Pandemic to Progress,* focuses in on seven of the skills that make the difference makers stand out from others! From the first page to the last page, Brian unpacks these observable skills and provides amazing stories and thoughts to go along with each of them. You are going to love this work from this amazing leader and friend. Brian has been given the great gift of observing and seeing what others may look past and then sharing insights that are life changing for you and me to learn and grow from! Even better, Brian himself lives each one of these out on a daily basis, which gives even more credibility to his work!

I cannot wait for you to dive into this great book and get sharpened by these seven skills! Trust me, this book will leave you better than it found you!

Mike Linch
Senior Pastor NorthStar Church
Podcast Host "Linch with a Leader"

Introduction

Jeff Struecker was an eighteen-year-old high school graduate with no plans for the future. He just knew college was not an option. A friend convinced him to speak to an Army recruiter. During the enlistment process, Jeff asked, "What's the toughest job in the Army?" After explaining the type of people Army Rangers were, the recruiter said, "Listen kid, you have no idea what you're asking for, and before you go any farther down this road, I want you to make sure you know what you're about to get into."

The reason Jeff wanted to join the Army Rangers was sobering. He wanted to go to combat and wanted to get shot at. You see, Jeff did not grow up in a church home, and he had an overwhelming fear of dying. This fear, which lasted for years, came from confusion over what happens the moment right after you die.

Growing up, he would often ask his parents about that moment, and they would say, "Jeff, after you die, you go to heaven. Everybody sits on clouds and plays a harp and everybody gets into heaven." Jeff would think about those answers, and it left him empty and scared. He knew there was an eternity out there, and he didn't know what to expect. This fear would often awake him during the middle of the night and lasted for years.

When Jeff was thirteen years old, a young couple in their twenties moved in just across the hall in the apartment complex his family was living in. Jeff not only became friends with the couple, they took him under their wing almost like you would a younger brother. After a few months, the couple took a courageous step and shared the Gospel of Jesus Christ with him. They explained to him who Jesus was. They talked about sin and what Jesus did on the cross. They said, "If you turn your life over to Jesus, He will radically change your life ... He will give you eternal life and you will never have to worry about what happens when you die." That night, Jeff prayed to receive Jesus and asked Him to change his life and remove his fear of dying. And Jesus did just that.

Now five years later, we return to Jeff's question about the toughest job in the Army. He proceeded to sign up for the Rangers because Jeff knew he would get shot at, and he wanted to truly know if he was ready to die. Fast forward to 1993 in Mogadishu, Somalia. The now Sergeant Struecker is part of the 75th Ranger Regiment and squad leader responsible for ten men. He is an experienced combatant, but the level of conflict in Somalia was nothing like he has seen before or since.

Special forces almost exclusively operate at night because they have a significant technological advantage. However, on Sunday October 3, 1993, two high-profile targets were discovered to be simultaneously located in the same building. Though not optimum, the time to move was going to be during daylight hours. The plan was for the soldiers to be lowered by ropes from Blackhawk helicopters and then secure the building. Sergeant Struecker's team would then drive up in three humvees and extract everyone involved and bring them safely back to base. But nothing ever goes according to plan.

Private First Class Todd Blackburn missed a rope and fell seventy feet to the streets below. Struecker's team had to then fight their way to him, load his stretcher on a middle vehicle, and then the unit's three vehicles would need to fight their way out of those streets and back to base. As they turned down one road, they were being assaulted by rocket grenades, hand grenades, and gunfire from every doorway, window, and rooftop. It was the worst assault Sergeant Struecker would ever experience in his military career. Getting back to the base was no longer the unit's top concern. It was simply getting to the next block.

When they finally returned to the base, Sergeant Struecker was advised a second Blackhawk had been shot down. The first Search and Rescue Force was already in the city streets. Regardless of the horror and danger they had just been through, Sergeant Struecker would have to go back out to help his comrades in harm's way. He then sent out a request for anyone who could assist. The response was overwhelming.

Cooks, intel analysts, supply clerks, and ammunition personnel all said they had guns and were ready to go. However, one of his men said, "Hey Sergeant, I can't go back out into those city streets tonight. I know if I get on those humvees with you, I'm going to die. I've got a wife at home and I know I'm going to die . . . I just can't do it." Sergeant Struecker pulled him to the side and said, "Look man, I'm scared, too, but I don't want you to think about yourself as a coward simply because you're afraid. You know the real difference between a hero and a coward? It's not fear. It's what you do with the fear. That's the difference. I need you on those humvees, and the guys on those city streets need you."

The most terrifying moment of Sergeant Struecker's life was hand-washing the already bloody humvee as he prepared to go back out. He knew it was a suicide mission. But he pledged his life to his friends, and he remembered the Ranger Creed that states "I will never leave a fallen comrade to fall into the hands of the enemy."

Overcome by fear, he prayed, "God, I know I'm in trouble. Tonight's the night I'm going to die, and I need your help." Sergeant Struecker then felt God saying, "Jeff, did you really trust me when you were thirteen years old? You said you believed but did you really? Because if you trusted me, I can take care you. I have you right in the palm on my hand. You don't have to worry about what happens next. I will take care of whatever happens to you next."

Sergeant Struecker still thought he was going to die, but things would only come down in one of two ways. One, maybe he survives and goes home to his family in Georgia. Two, if he were to die in the streets of Mogadishu, Somalia, before his body hits the ground, his soul would be with his Father in heaven. No matter what happens next, he could not lose. What Jesus Christ did on the cross 2,000 years ago was radically impacting his life right then in Mogadishu, Somalia.

The moments after the battle concluded were some of the most important moments of Sergeant Struecker's life. After safely returning to the hanger on October 5, 1993, before he could get back to his cot, fellow soldiers needed his immediate attention. They wanted to know what happened to their friends who had just died. They also wanted to know what would happen to them in similar circumstances. These were the exact same questions he was asking as a young child.

Sergeant Struecker began telling his fellow warriors about Jesus. He explained he could fight like he did because of his faith in Jesus, and his fellow soldiers needed that. Sergeant Struecker would soon go on to become an Army chaplain. As soldiers would head into combat, he would tell them, "I know (what you're facing) because I've been there. On the battlefield, it's different when your eternity is settled and your faith is in Jesus Christ."

For the last several decades, Sergeant Struecker has been both preparing for the enemy but also preparing his friends for eternity. Sergeant Struecker eventually planted a church just outside of Fort Benning, Georgia, so he "could reach America's warriors helping them get ready for eternity because some of them are going to meet Jesus face-to-face while they're young, and it's going to be because of a bullet on the battlefield."

This content came from a speech Sergeant Struecker gave to the men of Piedmont Church on October 4, 2022. That date just happened to be the twenty-ninth anniversary of his return from the streets of Mogadishu.

Jeff Struecker is many things:

- A skilled warrior
- Passionate
- Resilient
- A trusted teammate
- Content, at peace with himself, and loyal
- Brave
- And a man of great faith in Jesus Christ

Take a look at that list closely. It has more importance to you than you think. Sergeant Struecker's qualities may seem idealistic and old-fashioned, but after closer review, these traits are needed now more than ever. Understanding the implications of those seven qualities will be the difference between you achieving your full potential as a leader or not in a post-pandemic world.

If you are going to move from pandemic to progress, it will require you having these seven qualities. It will require that you become *mighty*. But the good news is that becoming mighty is possible for everyone, including you.

Jason Stoughton is a dear friend of mine. He is one of those individuals who has the gift of encouragement. Jason always has a huge smile on his face, is high-energy, and makes you feel like you are the most important person in the room. He is a member of John Maxwell's organization and brightens up every room with his positive attitude. Jason is the guy you call when you are having a bad day. He is a five-hour energy drink for your soul.

Jason and I were spending a few moments together at the Live 2 Lead Conference in October of 2021. He shared with me an idea he had about speaking on "moving people from pandemic to progress." I told him what a great concept it was. He laughed and said, "Now don't steal that idea." I smiled and assured him I would not. But as the next year progressed, I could not get his thought out of my mind. I finally called him and asked if he remembered our conversation. Jason laughed and said he did. I then inquired to see if he had done anything with the idea. He told me he had not.

I then said, "Jason, it's your idea but if I give you credit for it, can I use 'Pandemic to Progress' as part of my next book title and content." In true Jason Stoughton and John Maxwell fashion, he said, "Brian, if you think it will add value to people, then absolutely use it."

This book would not have been possible without my conversation with Jason from October 2021. He planted a seed into my mind about the type of people moving from pandemic to progress and the value they are adding to others. This most recent season of my life has been a deep dive into those who are succeeding when so much has been taken from them. I believe their stories and what we can learn from them unlocks the secrets needed to succeed in today's post-pandemic world.

So many people lost loved ones, opportunities, financial resources, careers, time, and much, much more during COVID. The worst thing many people lost was hope. COVID stripped away the non-essentials in our lives. It revealed how foolish pride, ego, and narcissism are. It made us question almost everything in our lives, including God himself. COVID brought us all to our knees in one form or fashion.

While certainly not the same, it reminded me of another great leader who had everything stripped from him. He was forced into isolation and brought to his knees as well. The leader's name is David. Yes, that David. King David. The great warrior and defeater of the giant Goliath.

Through no fault of his own, an up-and-coming David would fall out of favor with King Saul. Though he was a great warrior, winning many battles for the king and bringing him great comfort and enjoyment as his personal harp player, Saul hated David. This stemmed from Saul's jealousy of David's popularity and that he would one day replace him as king. Saul's jealousy and insecurity reached such a boiling point that on two separate occasions he launched a spear at David while playing the harp in hopes of killing him. Sadly, Saul was trying to murder the one who was comforting him.

Ultimately, David was forced to flee for his life. It was during this time from 1018 to 1014 BC when David was on the run that God began stripping away things from his life. Charles Swindoll in his wonderful book *David: A Story of Passion & Destiny* identified five "crutches" David had removed from his life.

First, David lost a significant leadership position in Saul's army. His efforts were heroic; but in an instant, he was no longer with the organization. Second, David lost a member of his family, his wife Michal. Michal just happened to be Saul's daughter. This marriage had been arranged as a result of his victory over Goliath. For his own personal safety, she had to be left behind as he fled.

Third, David lost emotional stability. David felt his own safety was at risk. In fact, in I Samuel 20:3 he said, "But truly, as the Lord lives and as your soul lives, there is but a step between me and death." Fourth, he lost close personal relationships. One example is his friendship with Jonathan, Saul's son. Jonathan was like a brother to David but much like Michal, their relationship became a casualty of the events beyond David's control. During this time, David also lost his relationship with his mentor Samuel.

Finally, Swindoll writes that David lost his self-respect. Seemingly without any options, David went to Gath. That's right Gath, home of the defeated Goliath. It is not possible in human words to express how despised David was in Gath. He was the source of their national embarrassment and the one who caused the most consequential defeat in their military history. But here was David, with great fear and trepidation, turning to those who hated him most for comfort and safety.

To make this possible, he acted as if he was afflicted with mental illness so they would take him in and not kill him. The Bible indicates David was literally foaming at the mouth. Eventually King Achish of Gath expelled him from his presence. He said, "Behold, you see the man is mad. Why then have you brought him to me? Do I lack madmen, that you have brought this fellow to behave as a madman in my presence?" (I Sam. 21:14-15).

If we were to compare the years of 1018–1014 BC for David, it would be similar to our 2020. Both were times when everything was stripped from our lives. Death was a constant reality. Many of you reading this book lost jobs and careers, lost your financial security, family members were socially distanced, or in the worst cases, sadly passed away. Friendships were strained or lost, and mental illnesses hit all-time highs.

But things eventually got better for David, and things are getting better for many today. But how? What are the skills you need to move from pandemic to progress? Let's return to David and a unique group of friends he made while on the run. First Samuel 22:2 tells us, "And everyone who was in distress, and everyone who was in debt, and everyone who was discontented, gathered to him; and he became captain over them. Now there were about four hundred men with him."

David took this ragtag group and formed them into a formidable fighting unit. In fact, a select group of thirty-seven men would form an elite unit which would become known as David's Mighty Men. It is from these Mighty Men, five in particular, in which we learn seven skills you need to move from pandemic to progress. You will notice these skills are quite similar to the ones exhibited by Sergeant Jeff Struecker. These seven skills are:

1. Production
2. Passion
3. Resilience
4. Teamwork
5. Contentment
6. Courage
7. Faith

The goal for everyone reading this book is to develop the skills to become mighty yourself. As you will discover, this is possible. You just need to develop the tools and mindset needed to do so.

As you read this book, it will remind you of my previous work *Timeless: 10 Enduring Practices of Apex Leaders*. I will construct a biblical framework for the skill followed by current examples of people utilizing it to become mighty and are moving from pandemic to progress.

Mighty: Seven Skills You Need to Move from Pandemic to Progress is also the sequel to my previous book *2021 The Year in Leadership* as the vast majority of my examples are from the year of 2022. This is comforting because this book is not theory. It contain real-life stories and lessons from those who are becoming mighty and going from the pandemic to progress right now.

This book is not intended to be read alone. *Mighty* can have broader applications in your leadership. For churches, it can serve as a seven-week sermon series or seven-week small group curriculum. For those in the business, athletic, or nonprofit world, *Mighty* would be an ideal resource to equip and inspire your teams. Do a chapter a week together. And before giving any public address, let this book be a resource of great stories and content you can use to inspire others.

At the end of each chapter is a set of discussion questions for you to answer individually and collectively with your team. You get to grow and become mighty together!

If you feel everything has been stripped from you and things appear hopeless, be encouraged because they have not. Things were not hopeless for David while on he was on the run in the wilderness, and things are not hopeless for you now. By implementing the principles contained in this book, you, too, can become mighty and move from pandemic to progress.

Let's get started!

CHAPTER 1

Production

> "These are the names of the mighty men whom David had: Josheb-basshebeth a Tahchemonite; he was chief of the three. He wielded his spear against eight hundred whom he killed at one time."
>
> —2 Samuel 23:8 (ESV)

From Josheb-basshebeth, we learn that those who wish to become mighty and move from pandemic to progress are people of production. They get things done. It is production, the fulfillment of vision, the fact you told people about a brighter tomorrow and it actually came to pass, that ultimately makes you a leader worth following. As you read about this man, you get a sense he was like a comic book Avenger during his day. Josheb-basshebeth literally killed eight-hundred men at one time with a spear.

I try to imagine what this moment must have been like. I mentally insert myself into the story and pretend Josheb-basshebeth and I are friends traveling through the countryside. Either we suddenly stumble upon this army, are seeking them out (we are warriors after all), or we walk into an ambush. There was a great likelihood the chief of the fugitive David's Mighty Men had a hefty bounty on his head. In any event, Josheb-basshebeth and I are now face-to-face with eight hundred men wanting to kill him.

This army was likely licking their chops because of how outnumbered Josheb-basshebeth was. They were probably expecting an unconditional surrender. Threats of torture and forced servitude were surely being yelled out. The worst possible outcome was that Josheb-basshebeth was about to become a trophy kill, with his head literally served up on a platter. Things appeared hopeless.

It is the midst of this dire situation, I imagine Josheb-basshebeth calmly looks at me and says, "Back up. You will want to get behind me." In sheer terror, I immediately do more than just back up. I retreat about fifty yards and hide behind the largest tree or rock I can find. Then to my amazement, I watch this BC-era Avenger go to work and begin slaying soldier after soldier. Oftentimes, multiple soldiers were put down simultaneously. As fast as the enemy approached, they fell even faster. Though this was a violent and bloody scene, there are three things I noticed about this mighty warrior and why he was so productive.

Elite Training
Breathtaking Health
Highly Efficient

To become mighty and move from pandemic to progress, you will need all three as well. Let's take a look at each.

- ELITE TRAINING -

TOM MULLINS

Tom Mullins is the founding pastor of Christ Fellowship Church in Palm Beach Gardens, Florida. Prior to leading one of America's greatest churches, Mullins was a very successful high school and college football coach. Even as a pastor, he is still called Coach Mullins to this very day. I had the opportunity to be part of a group of approximately thirty individuals who were privileged to receive special instruction from this amazing leader. Coach Mullins concluded our time by sharing what he has learned that allows leaders to truly make a difference and stand out from all others.

While coaching Georgetown College (KY) in 1977, Coach Mullins arranged for his staff to join him in spending several days at the training camps of the Ohio State Buckeyes and Cincinnati Bengals. They witnessed everything these elite programs did from drills to strength and conditioning to nutrition to practice schedules. Afterward, Coach Mullins and his staff began to download what they learned and figure out how they could best apply those lessons to their own team.

Coach Mullins said, "We were doing the same things they (Ohio State and Cincinnati) were doing. The differences were they were bigger and stronger than we were and they executed the fundamentals more consistently and at an elite level." He then concluded with the primary lesson for all leaders to apply, "It's all about the consistency of the execution of the fundamentals which make us stand out."

From Coach Mullins's experience, we learn a couple of leadership lessons. For the most part, all leaders have access to the same information. But the best leaders take that information and create an individualized training plan to get better. But most importantly, the difference between professionals and amateurs, regardless of your profession, is the consistent execution of the fundamentals of their craft.

Do you want to truly make a difference as a leader and stand out from all others? I'm sure you do which is why you are reading this book. Then make a commitment right now to consistently execute the fundamentals of your craft at the highest level possible. This will help you become Mighty and move from pandemic to progress.

JIRO ONO

Let's now transition from a great pastor and coach to the person recognized as the world's greatest sushi chef, Jiro Ono. His restaurant, Sukiyabashi Jiro, has received the prestigious Michelin Guide's top three-star status from 2007 to 2019. President Obama has even dined at his restaurant.

As told in Ryan Hawk's excellent book *The Pursuit Of Excellence: The Uncommon Behaviors of the World's Most Productive Achievers*, what makes his story fascinating is the restaurant is located in a subway station in Tokyo and can only seat ten people at a time. Ono, who is ninety-six years old, has been preparing sushi for over seventy years. Because of his legendary status within the industry, Ono was the subject of the documentary, *Jiro Dreams of Sushi*.

When asked how he became the best in world, Ono gave the secret to his success. He said, "Once you decide on your occupation, you must immerse yourself in your work. You have to fall in love with your work. Never complain about your job. You must dedicate your life to mastering your skill. That is the secret to success."

Ono added, "All I want to do is to make better sushi. I do the same thing over and over, improving it bit by bit. There is always a yearning to achieve more. I'll continue to climb, trying to reach the top, but no one knows where the top is. I've never once hated this job and gave my life to it. . . . Even at my age, after decades of work, I don't think I have achieved perfection."

As I read the comments of this legendary culinarian genius in light of the production of Josheb-basshebeth, I gleaned five things required to master your craft:

First, mastering your craft requires a decision. Ono said, "Once you decide on your occupation." While it is good to experiment with different jobs early in your career, there comes a time you must commit to something if you ever want to produce superior results. Indecisiveness or a lack of commitment will eventually derail your efforts toward mastering your craft.

Second, mastering your craft also requires complete immersion. Those who master their craft are not part-time or "dipping their toes in the water." They are all-in. Ono noted, "You must immerse yourself in your work. You have to fall in love with your work. Never complain about your job. You must dedicate your life to mastering your skill."

Third, to achieve mastery you must have a singular focus, a "this one thing I do" type of mentality. There cannot be a number of competing interests in your life. Ono added, "All I want to do is to make better sushi." How many things do you want to do in your life? If the answer is many, you will not likely achieve mastery or have high production.

Fourth, mastering your craft requires improved repetition. This type of repetition is not just focused on developing muscle memory or getting in your 10,000 hours. It is doing the same thing over and over again with an eye on self-evaluation and constant improvement. Ono continued, "I do the same thing over and over, improving it bit by bit."

Finally, mastering your craft is an oval track with no finish line. You never truly arrive as a leader. It is similar to accumulating knowledge. The more you know, the more you realize you don't know. Ono is the greatest sushi chef in the world and, at ninety-six years old, has an insatiable desire to improve. He concluded, "There is always a yearning to achieve more. I'll continue to climb, trying to reach the top, but no one knows where the top is. . . . Even at my age, after decades of work, I don't think I have achieved perfection."

If the most decorated sushi chef in the world with seventy years of experience feels he can improve, then surely you and I should have the humility to admit we can as well.

RAFAEL NADAL

You may not know who Toni Nadal is but you certainly have heard of his famous nephew, legendary tennis superstar Rafael Nadal, winner of twenty-one Grand Slam titles. Toni became Rafael's coach when he was just eight-years-old. His no-nonsense disciplined approach became a critical component in his nephew's success. Uncle Toni was happy to coach and train Rafael but had a few ground rules. These ground rules give a template all up-and-coming leaders should be willing to follow if they wish to become mighty.

First, Rafael needed to learn respect. Toni told Rafael, "If you ever throw a racket, we're finished. They're expensive, and when you throw a racket, you don't just disrespect the sport, you disrespect all the people who can't afford equipment." What a great way to fight a sense of entitlement in a young leader's life.

Second, Rafael needed to learn accountability. This is one of the most difficult things for young leaders to learn. In fact, it is difficult for any leader, regardless of age. Toni added, "Losing is part of competing. You will lose. And when you lose, it's not going to be my fault or the fault of your racket or the balls or the courts or the weather. It is your fault, and you will accept it. Too many people in this world make excuses for their problems. You take responsibility and try and do better next time. That's all." Losing is part of competing. What a great lesson!

Third, Rafael needed to learn how to have fun and then how to leverage it. Not only do leaders have to learn how to properly handle failure, but they also need to learn how to effectively steward the good times. Toni continued, "Have fun. When you stop enjoying this, it's not good. You'll find something else that gives you pleasure." Fun is the fuel that gives us the impetus to continue moving forward as leaders. Furthermore, a leader who does not celebrate or have fun is a leader not worth following.

Finally, Rafael needed to learn the value of hard work. At only eight years old, Rafael had just won the under-twelve division for the country of Spain. Looking at the list of previous champions, Toni asked the young prodigy, "How many names do you recognize?" Rafael replied with a shrug, "Not many." Toni then said, "Exactly." It was a reminder that winning a junior title meant nothing in regard to long-term success. Toni was reminding Rafael he must continue to work hard and continually improve moving forward.

As a young leader, you may have all the talent in the world. But if you don't learn respect, accountability, how to leverage fun, and the value of hard work, your success will be limited at best, and you will never become mighty and move from pandemic to progress.

BRYCE YOUNG

Alabama Crimson Tide head coach Nick Saban is not one to give out compliments easily. But after the team's 20–19 victory over the Texas Longhorns on September 10, 2022, he was overly generous with praise when asked about another young leader, his star quarterback and Heisman Trophy winner Bryce Young.

In a postgame news conference Coach Saban said, "The guy studies. He prepares well for the game. He understands exactly what the defense is in and what they're going to do. He understands protections; he knows how to protect himself. (He) knows when he's got to throw the ball hot. He's athletic enough to extend plays and make plays. He's accurate throwing the ball, and he's very, very instinctive. He plays quarterback like a point guard in basketball. He's got talent, but he just doesn't just play with his talent. He's very well-prepared and knows exactly what the game plan is and what he needs to do to execute it."

So what would make Coach Saban, who comes across as someone who is rarely satisfied with anyone or anything, hand out so many plaudits? Here's what leaders who wish to be mighty can learn from Coach Saban's comments about Bryce Young:

He is humble and a continual learner. Young understands the value of training and preparation and is knowledgeable of his industry. He is smart and makes quick decisions which produce positive results. Young does not make unnecessary mistakes, which allows the organization to have sustainability. Finally, he does not just rely on his talent. Young has great intuition and executes the team's plans at an elite level.

As a leader, could we say the same things about you? If so, you might even impress Nick Saban himself. Another young leader trying to become mighty in 2022 was New York Jets quarterback Zach Wilson. Unfortunately, he left a different impression than Young.

ZACH WILSON

Wilson was selected by the Jets with the second overall pick in the 2021 NFL Draft. Since then, Wilson has faced a series of challenges both on and off the field. Now in his second season, many experts have expressed concern about his ability to lead the Jets into the future.

For instance, on the November 3, 2022 edition of *The Herd With Colin Cowherd*, NFL Films analyst Greg Cosell said the following:

"The film shows he doesn't see the field with the needed clarity at this point. I think he needs to settle down as a pocket quarterback. A couple of the things stand out on film: he's too lazy and slow with his drop and set into the pocket. That needs to get quicker. He's much too reactive to what he perceives as pressure but (it) is not pressure by NFL standards. So he needs to develop a far better sense of pocket-feel and presence. He's too frenetic; he moves too much. His feet, while they're really light and athletic, need to settle down. So, he has a ways to go in that regard. Now, he shows flashes. We know he's got a whippy arm. We know he can make throws. We know on occasion that he'll make a special throw because he's that kind of talent. But the details of the position really need work and right now he's a little bit of a chaotic player."

Cosell's analysis of Wilson may sound harsh, but he has been breaking down film and analyzing players for NFL Films since 1984. For thirty-eight years, Cosell has been one of the most respected evaluators in football. He knows what he is talking about.

The following are six things we learn from Cosell's evaluation of Wilson that young leaders need to do to become highly productive in their area of discipline. For Wilson, it is quarterbacking a professional football team. For you, it will be something else probably much less high-profile. Regardless of the industry, these skills are vital to becoming mighty and moving from pandemic to progress.

First, young leaders need to develop clarity about their lives and what is needed to be as productive as possible. Cosell said, "He doesn't see the field with the needed clarity at this point." Second, young leaders need to remain calm. Cosell noted, "I think he needs to settle down as a pocket quarterback." Cosell later adds, "So he needs to develop a far better sense of pocket-feel and presence. He's too frenetic; he moves too much. His feet, while they're really light and athletic, need to settle down. So, he has a ways to go in that regard."

Third, and might I add this will cause you to quickly lose the respect of seasoned leaders, young leaders need to develop a sense of urgency and professional work ethic. This is critical to being as productive as possible. Cosell observed, "A couple of the things stand out on film, he's too lazy and slow with his drop and set into the pocket. That needs to get quicker." Fourth, young leaders need to learn how to properly evaluate pressure and how to effectively handle it. Not only do you not want to be seen as lazy, you want to avoid being known for lacking resilience and mental stamina as well. We will dedicate an entire chapter to this topic later in the book. But Cosell lamented, "He's much too reactive to what he perceives as pressure, but (it) is not pressure by NFL standards."

But one thing young leaders can immediately do to have positive production is to identify and develop their strengths. Cosell noted, "Now, he shows flashes. We know he's got a whippy arm. We know he can make throws. We know on occasion that he'll make a special throw because he's that kind of talent." And sixth, young leaders need to master the fundamentals of their profession. Cosell concluded, "But the details of the position really need work, and right now he's a little bit of a chaotic player."

Do you have any young leaders in your organization you are developing? If so, which of these six areas do they need to work on?

DAK PRESCOTT

But what happens when the training and development you have had is insufficient? For example, let's look at Dallas Cowboys quarterback Dak Prescott. On January 16, 2022, the Dallas Cowboys were on the San Francisco 49ers' 41-yard line with fourteen seconds left to play with no timeouts remaining. Trailing 23–17, Prescott was driving the team toward a potential winning touchdown and miraculous comeback.

After taking the snap from center, Prescott performed a quarterback draw and began running down the middle of the field, rather than to the sidelines to stop the clock. With only seven seconds remaining, he slid down at the 24-yard line. The clock continued to run as players from both teams frantically lined up for the game's final play.

Rather than a standard end-of-the-game situation, this became a worse-case scenario for the Cowboys. The referee began to spot the ball at the line of scrimmage with only two seconds remaining. Before Prescott could take the snap and have an opportunity for a final pass into the end zone, the clock ran out, showing 00:00 time remaining. The referee then announced six words which will live in Cowboys infamy, "That's the end of the game."

The 49ers celebrated. The Cowboys were in shock. The fans in attendance were aghast. Twitter exploded, and a media firestorm ensued. The following morning, ESPN's Dan Orlovsky and Rex Ryan discussed the Cowboys' inefficiencies with great fervor on the network's *Get Up* program. Orlovsky's analysis provided great insight into how to properly handle worse-case scenarios.

It has often been said that crisis does not create character, it reveals it. Crisis also reveals a person or team's training, situational awareness, and ability to execute under pressure. Orlovsky said, "This play is about the Cowboys' lack of awareness and lack of execution."

Proving his point, the Cowboys showed a lack of understanding of their field position and the time remaining on the clock. Orlovsky noted, "At some point you have to declare yourself down because the extra two-to-three yards is not worth it because it's going to take an extra second or two." Ryan added, "It's not about getting into a spot to spike the football but to run a play. That certainly wasn't on the minds of the Dallas Cowboys."

While worse-case scenarios can reveal a lack of training, awareness, and ability to execute under pressure, they also shine a light on the top thing a leader must do to successfully handle those situations. Orlovsky said, "How many times did they practice it not working ideally? . . . When your blood pressure is up and it's the moment, how many times did they prepare for the worst-case scenario? That's what it looked like to me that they didn't prepare for the worst-case scenario."

I have trained many people. You may have, as well. Most training is for ideal situations. It is to give a person the fundamental skills necessary to carry out a minimum task or assignment under perfect conditions. Most training does not prepare a person for any complexity or worst-case scenarios. This is the question Orlovsky was asking. Did their training prepare the Cowboys and Dak Prescott for this moment? Most observers think not. They look at the team's play-calling, clock management, substitution patterns, lack of urgency, and Prescott handing the ball to the center rather than the referee at the end of the game as evidence of their concerns.

To alleviate any concerns your organization may have in your leadership during moments of crisis, the number one thing you can do to increase productivity is constantly train and practice for worst-case or high-pressure scenarios.

Create difficult and stressful situations for your team in training. Apply pressure in training situations so they will feel less pressure in real life. Make mistakes in practice, not in the game. You want to put people in actual situations where they can mess up in a safe environment and then learn from their experience. Smart leaders practice crisis situations so often that proper behavior in those instances becomes second nature.

Orlovsky concluded by saying, "I (Cowboys owner Jerry Jones) pay you as a coach to be ready for the moment, and I pay you as a quarterback to be elite in the moment and neither of those happened." Let's now take a look at someone whose lack of training for an unexpected event can mean the difference not between winning and losing, but between life and death.

NEPALESE SHERPA KAMI RITA

As of May 6, 2022, Mount Everest had been climbed 10,657 times since Sir Edmund Hillary first made the trek in 1953. The person who has climbed the 29,032-foot mountain the most times is a Nepalese Sherpa by the name of Kami Rita. Over the weekend of May 6, 2022, Rita scaled Everest for a record twenty-sixth time.

Sherpas are often referred to as the guardian angels of the Himalayas. They provide a myriad of services for those wishing to scale Mount Everest. In addition to being guides up the mountain, they also set up basecamp, act as porters, and keep the hikers safe at all points along the journey.

Whether you lead a church, business, athletic organization, or nonprofit, there are several leadership lessons we learn from Kami Rita and his fellow Sherpas about being highly productive people who also set and break records:

First, record-breaking leaders are first and foremost servants. Mark 10:45 says, "For even the Son of Man came not to be served but to serve, and to give his life as a ransom for many." The only successful leadership model is servant leadership. No one is more skilled at climbing or has more knowledge of Everest than experienced Sherpas. Yet, these gifted climbers humbly serve those who employ their services by doing seemingly menial tasks to help them scale the mountain.

Second, record-breaking leaders know the way. There is a difference between exposure and experience. When going into unknown terrain or somewhere you've never been before, you want to go with someone who knows the way. I once heard John Maxwell explain the difference between a travel agent and a tour guide. A travel agent has exposure but not experience. They say, "Here's a brochure. Isn't this a pretty picture? Here's where it is located on the map. I hear great things about this place."

But a tour guide has experience from being on the ground. A tour guide says, "Here are the places you really want to go. These are the best places to eat. If you really want to have fun, go here. It's not on the normal tour." Sherpas know the best way to head up the mountain. They take their parties to the places with the best views. Sherpas have the experience to give others memorable experiences. Similarly, great leaders know the best way to lead their teams because they have been where their teams are trying to go.

Third, record-breaking leaders plan for contingencies. Mount Everest is not an easy climb; it puts up a fight. There are constantly changing weather conditions and shifting terrain, which can alter the expedition and even put people in physical danger. A great Sherpa is an expert at navigating these unforeseen events. A great leader is also an expert at navigating unforeseen events as well.

Fourth, record-breaking leaders help others reach the top. Sherpas help others reach the top of the mountain. In helping others reach the pinnacle of their professions, leaders help others reach the top as well. Smart leaders learn what their team members laugh about, cry about, and dream about. And then do everything within their power to make those dreams become reality.

Josheb-basshebeth was immediately thrust into crisis and performed at an elite level, killing eight-hundred men with only a spear. Because of his training and preparation, he was not only ready for the moment but mighty in it.

Leaders, you have been asked to be ready for worst-case and high-pressure scenarios and perform at an elite level in those moments as well. Have you trained for those situations so that you will be prepared when the time comes? If not, start preparing for them today. Another unexpected worst-case situation took place on the morning of Friday, December 16, 2002.

AQUADOM

Previously, on December 2, 2003, the AquaDom was opened in the Radisson Collection Hotel in Berlin, Germany at the cost of 12.8 million euros. Located in the hotel's lobby, it was an architectural marvel. The AquaDom was an eighty-two-feet acrylic glass aquarium with approximately 1,500 fish, representing over 1,000 species. Furthermore, it contained an inside transparent elevator allowing hotel guests to enjoy being literally on the inside of the aquarium itself. The AquaDom held the Guinness World Record as the world's largest cylindrical aquarium.

You may have noticed in the previous paragraph I frequently used terms like *was* and *held*. This was not by accident.

At 5:45 a.m. on Friday, December 16, the aquarium burst, spilling 264,172 gallons of water and marine life across the building's lobby and into the streets outside. All 350 of hotel guests had to be evacuated. More than 100 firefighters were dispatched to the hotel for an event so significant seismographs picked up the catastrophe. Few if any fish were expected to survive. The reason for the aquarium's collapse is still being investigated at the time of this writing.

Analyzing this incident from a leadership perspective would lead you to talk about things like how a crisis can happen at a moment's notice or how a person can become suddenly overwhelmed with problems in their life and leadership. While those may be true, I think they provide a limited menu of what we can learn from the AquaDom.

I think the greater lesson is, while you may be personally or corporately setting records, producing significant results, feeling bulletproof, and think you are insulated from failure and have it all under control, this feeling of control is only a mirage. The AquaDom is a reminder for leaders to stay humble, remain diligent, keep working hard, and remember the behaviors and practices that got you where you are. No matter what level of success you may be experiencing, stay true to your training and fundamentals. Because if you don't, when you least expect it, at 5:45 a.m. while you are asleep, your leadership or organization could unexpectedly collapse just like the AquaDom.

- BREATHTAKING HEALTH -

The second reason why I feel Josheb-basshebeth was so productive was his health. I have had the misfortune of seeing two grown men have a physical altercation. I'm not talking about professional combat sports like mixed martial arts or professional boxing. I'm talking about socially dysfunctional parents at a baseball game arguing over whether someone was out or not and ultimately having a fight.

After watching this specific incident in person and dozens of videos on YouTube and media outlets, I have two practical takeaways. First, it appears most nonprofessional fights between adults last less than ten seconds. Usually, the first person who lands a punch wins as the other retreats or is incapacitated. My second observation is how physically exhausted they are after their confrontation. Perhaps it is because of the rush of adrenalin, but both individuals, the winner and loser, are exhausted.

As I imagine Josheb-basshebeth defeating eight-hundred men, one after the other after the other, his physical and competitive stamina are astonishing. Josheb-basshebeth never gets tired. Josheb-basshebeth is in shape. He has great endurance. Josheb-basshebeth has taken care of his body, and the results are bearing this out.

If you are going to be a highly productive person, you have to take care of yourself physically. To prove my point, allow me to give you a humorous but very practical example.

On June 2, 2021, TNT analyst Charles Barkley coined a nickname for Los Angeles Lakers forward Anthony Davis by referring to him as "Street Clothes." Barkley called Davis "Street Clothes" because he is often injured, sitting on the team's bench in his street clothes, and unable to play for his team.

In a February 5, 2022 article on Marca.com, Dr. Jurdan Mendiguchia made an interesting observation, "There's this premise that the success of player depends on ability, which is made up of technical, physical, tactical and psychological aspects, and that this is then multiplied by their availability."

The world-renowned physiotherapist then added, "Many (soccer) players have told me that Arjen Robben could have been close to Cristiano Ronaldo or Lionel Messi in ability, but he didn't make it because he didn't have much availability."

What we learn from Anthony Davis, Dr. Mendiguchia, and Arjen Robben is what experienced leaders already know. The three greatest abilities a leader has are the following:

1. Availability
2. Dependability
3. Reliability

A person may have elite talent like Davis and Robben. They may have all the potential in the world. We may have been seduced by their skills and dreamt of what our organization could become with them at full-strength. But we just could not depend on them to be there when needed. Their availability was suspect and as a result, they were unreliable.

Every leadership ability—people skills, strategic thinking, communication skills, team building, vision, etc.—is built upon the foundations of availability, dependability, and reliability. Everything flows from these three abilities.

If you do not possess these three things beyond ability, you can't be on the team. I'm sorry, but trust becomes lost because people simply can't count on you. You have become "Street Clothes." As a result, they are forced to replace you with someone they can rely upon.

THE BROOKLYN NETS

Prior to the 2021–2022 season, many people predicted the Brooklyn Nets, with superstar players Kevin Durant, James Harden, and Kyrie Irving, would represent the Eastern Conference in the NBA Finals. But it was not to be so.

Harden would be traded while Durant and Irving missed twenty-seven and fifty-three games respectively. The team's dysfunctional season ended in embarrassing fashion as the Nets were swept 4–0 by the Boston Celtics. Much of the blame is falling on Irving for his selfishness, consistently sitting out of games throughout the season and its effect on team chemistry. Irving being unreliable is nothing new. During his eleven-year career, he has missed 281 games or 31.5 percent of his team's games.

In a May 11 post-season news conference, the team's general manager Sean Marks addressed Irving's professionalism saying, "We're looking for guys that want to come in here and be part of something bigger than themselves, play selfless, play team basketball, and be available. That goes not only for Kyrie but for everybody here."

He added, "Whenever you have a key part of your team that isn't available and you're trying to build chemistry, you're trying to build camaraderie out on the court I think it's very difficult." Marks then reiterated, "We need people here that want to be here, that are selfless, that want to be part of something bigger than themselves. There's an objective and there's a goal at stake here. In order to do that, we're going to need availability from everybody."

The Kyrie Irving saga once again reminds us of the three most important abilities a leader has—*dependability*, *availability*, and *reliability*. Maybe being swept by the Celtics has caused the Nets to finally come to the place where they have decided Irving can no longer be on their team. He is just not dependable, available, or reliable. Are you?

As a leader, you simply cannot take people where you are physically unable to go yourself. Quality health protects your leadership. It allows you to continue leading day after day, year after year. Your excellent health will help others reach the top as well. But if your health goes, so does your leadership.

PAUL O'NEILL, CEO OF ALCOA

Many business leaders have discovered the impact of physical health on their company's bottom line and overall culture. One such leader is Paul O'Neill, former CEO of Alcoa. When O'Neill became CEO of Alcoa in 1987, the company was facing significant challenges. Wall Street had serious concerns about the company's revenue projections and profit margins. In his first address to shareholders, O'Neill did little to install confidence a turnaround was possible. In fact, it was quite the opposite.

In what would become a legendary speech in business circles, O'Neill said, "I want to talk to you about worker safety." Worker safety? Of all the issues he could talk about, worker safety? Investors immediately began selling off their shares.

O'Neill attempted to ease their concerns by reasoning, "If you want to understand how Alcoa is doing, you need to look at our workplace safety figures. If we bring our injury rates down, it won't be because of cheerleading or the nonsense you sometimes hear from other CEOs. It will be because the individuals at this company have agreed to become part of something important: They've devoted themselves to creating a habit of excellence."

Organizational leaders can learn the following from O'Neill's "how you do anything is how you do everything" approach:

- Successful leaders are laser-focused on the key success links of the organization.

- Smart leaders are data driven.

- Even smarter leaders know which data is most important and how to leverage that information.

- Cheerleading moves emotions but rarely the bottom line. Standards move the bottom line.

- There is a lot of nonsense being done by leaders.

- One of the goals of leadership is to create something "bigger than myself" which people can buy into.

- Successful organizations have created a culture of excellence.

- Successful organizations know worker safety and other health items are reflective of your culture of excellence.

What were the results of O'Neill's efforts? When he retired after thirteen years as Alcoa's CEO and chairman, the company's net income increased 500 percent! If you are looking to become a successful leader, the lessons learned from O'Neill's time at Alcoa provide you a quality template.

I wish I had a Paul O'Neill earlier in my life, and because I didn't, I am usually not too hard on Anthony Davis, Kyrie Irving, or Arjen Robbin. I could have been called "Street Clothes" myself.

In June 2021, I was attending the Southern Baptist Convention in Nashville, Tennessee. In the midst of all the political fireworks taking place at the event, I was hoping to build relationships with key influencers in the church construction and finance space.

The conference was in a main session, and I wanted to use that time to speak with vendors. There were approximately seventy-five different booths and displays, but located in the center of the exhibit hall was a medical area provided by *Guidepost*. It had approximately a dozen stations where you could check your medical vital signs. The physicians would check your height and weight, and then walk you through a quick battery of tests for heart rate, blood pressure, and blood sugar.

I had been feeling quite tired recently. This was not a concern for me as I just wrote it off as a stressful season in my life. I thought, "Hey, I don't want to be found dead in a hotel room, so I'll take a couple of minutes and get my vitals checked while everyone else is in the conference." My flippant response would soon prove to be short-sighted and foolish.

I sat down with a very nice lady who was going through the normal procedures. She asked my name, date of birth, and how I was enjoying the event. We were going through a normal process when suddenly she got a concerned look on her face. She then asked, "Mr. Dodd, do you feel well?" I said, "Well, I'm a little tired, but yeah, I feel fine." Her response was straight-forward and direct, "Mr. Dodd, I'd like for you to see the doctor." At this point, I was escorted from my seat in the public area to behind a private curtain where I met with a doctor.

He asked, "Mr. Dodd, do you feel well?" This was the second time I had been asked this question in less than a minute. I responded, "Well, yeah I'm a little tired. It's a crazy season at work, and I just want to make sure I don't die in a hotel room in a city far from home, but yeah, I feel fine." He said, "Mr. Dodd, do you have someone who can drive you home?" I said, "No, I'm here by myself just working the event. Why?"

The doctor then said the words which would forever change the rest of my life. "Mr. Dodd, your blood sugar is 368. Normal blood sugar is seventy to ninety-nine. I don't even know how you're still standing. You should go to the emergency room right now." I finished up a little work I had left to do and then started my four-hour drive home.

I-24 is a long stretch of road between Nashville and Chattanooga. It was halfway through this drive that I mustered up the courage to call my wife Sonya and give her the bad news. She became very upset and emotional, but I assured her I was fine. We decided to meet at the emergency room of our local hospital. While there, my blood sugar had already dropped in half, but I was advised I had adult-onset diabetes. A meeting was scheduled with an endocrinologist the following morning. Life would never be the same again.

Here is why my personal health is so tied to my personal productivity. Sales is a large part of my daily responsibilities. People with diabetes are subject to blindness and heart attacks. If I ever suffered from either of those, blindness or heart attacks, how many sales do you think I would be able to make? That's right, zero!

Even worse beyond the numbers is I could potentially no longer be available, dependable, or reliable to my organization. There could be some long-term disability involved, but eventually, they would have to move on.

Your productivity can recover from a number of things with intentionality, experience, more opportunity, or better training. It cannot recover from a failure in health. People who are mighty and moving from pandemic to progress focus on maintaining a healthy lifestyle.

- HIGHLY EFFICIENT -

People who are highly productive have elite training, breathtaking health, and are also highly efficient. Going back to my mind's eye and witnessing Josheb-basshebeth's heroics, one thing I noticed was there is no wasted energy. Every movement had intentionality. Faced with the task of killing eight hundred enemy combatants, he was forced to edit his life and remove anything which prevented his success. His very life depended on it.

Each week I have the privilege of being part of a Zoom Bible study with dozens of high school, college, and professional baseball coaches and scouts from across the country. It is my favorite forty-five minutes of the week. One evening, many were in town for a tournament at a local sports complex. The Bible study's leader, Pastor Mike Linch of NorthStar Church, invited me and those who were in town to his home for dinner.

One of my favorite conversations of the evening was with Coach Marlin McPhail, former professional player and long-time scout of the New York Mets. Coach McPhail passionately loves Jesus and baseball. I learned a lot about leadership listening to this wonderful man.

Our group discussed several topics, but what I enjoyed most was an impromptu hitting lesson he gave. He is a coach, after all! Coach McPhail said, "When a hitter leans backwards in the batter's box, that's a no-no." He then went on to demonstrate that when you lean back, you have to shift your weight forward to gain proper balance, and then redirect your weight forward to hit the ball. This is highly inefficient. You should simply begin in proper balance, so you can direct all your energy toward the forward motion of hitting the ball.

As I listened to Coach McPhail, I was reminded of a quote I read in Pol Ballus and Lu Martin's book *Pep's City: The Making of a Superteam* about Manchester City's manager Pep Guardiola and the championship team he constructed.

They wrote, "Pep casts a beady eye over today's weigh-in results. Every player has been given detailed instructions regarding diet and weight, carefully calibrated by the club dietician according to height and muscle mass. Pep's a stickler in this regard and there'll be no mercy for anyone who has failed to stick to the agreed parameters."

What we learn from Coaches McPhail and Guardiola is a primary difference between ordinary and extraordinary leaders, teams, and overall performance is daily attention to detail.

Little things make a big difference. Small things compounded over time add up to huge results. Sometimes it's leaning back in batter's box or a daily adherence to nutrition, which separates ordinary from extraordinary athletes. The difference between ordinary and extraordinary really is just a little extra.

Have faith that the compounding results will come from doing just a little extra day-after-day will show up. Don't take shortcuts. Pay attention to the details. Do the little things well. Be efficient. Trust your training. If you do, you too will likely begin to see greater results sooner rather than later.

KANSAS CITY CHIEFS

Contrary to popular belief, leaders cannot simply "will their way" to great productivity. They need certain factors around them in order to be successful.

On Sunday, October 24, 2021, the Kansas City Chiefs were soundly defeated by the Tennessee Titans 27–3. Despite having the game's best player in quarterback Patrick Mahomes, the Chiefs had a record of 3–4 at the time. Mahomes was struggling and had thrown five interceptions in the previous three games. Changes were needed for the Chiefs collectively, and Mahomes specifically, to regain lost momentum.

As reported by Philadelphia Eagles president Joe Banner and Ben Eisner on the wonderful website The33rdTeam.com, head coach Andy Reid began making several schematic changes to help his young leader be more successful. In short, he simplified the offense and became more efficient.

First, Reid played to his team's strengths. All successful leaders have "go-to's" when things get tough, things they can count on. Reid's go-to throughout his career has been the quick passing game. Banner said, "When things aren't going well, Reid falls back on the screen. I've seen him do it before. He is running a ridiculous number of screens, including screens to RBs, WRs, TEs."

After reading Banner's comments, take a moment as a leader and determine what is it that you fall back on? What's your go-to?

Second, trust your teammates. To regain lost momentum, leaders must have the self-awareness to know they can't do it all by themselves. They must take advantage of their talented teammates. Instead of relying on Mahomes to make big plays down the field, Reid's play-calling became focused on quickly getting the ball out of his hands and into the hands of the team's many playmakers.

Finally, remove all obstacles from those on your team which may prevent them from being successful. When you have talented team members, your organization has a responsibility to put them in the best possible positions to succeed. Getting the ball to the playmakers as quickly as possible allowed them to be in open space (fewer defenders) and use their superior athleticism to gain yards after the catch.

After making these three schematic changes—playing to your strengths, trusting your talented teammates, and removing any obstacles preventing them from being successful—the Kansas City Chiefs won their next eight consecutive games and came within one game of going to their third consecutive Super Bowl. If your team is currently not efficient or successful, implement these three practices and watch productivity increase.

SUPER BOWL LVI

The team that defeated the Chiefs and went onto Super Bowl LVI was the Cincinnati Bengals. The three lessons we learn about productivity from Josheb-basshebeth—elite training, breathtaking health, and high efficiency—all came together and crystallized when the Bengals faced the Los Angeles Rams in America's largest sporting event.

The Rams would defeat the Bengals 23–20 in a game viewed by 112.3 million people, a 14 percent increase over the previous year. What they witnessed was a game filled with multiple leadership lessons.

First, if you want to get better as an organization, get a better leader. The previous off-season, the Los Angeles Rams acquired quarterback Matthew Stafford via trade. Two years prior, the Cincinnati Bengals had drafted their franchise quarterback Joe Burrow. Now each was in the Super Bowl. The primary difference between these teams today and where they were previously are their leaders, Stafford and Burrow.

If you have a department in your organization which is underperforming, the solution is likely getting a better leader. Upgrading the leadership position certainly worked for the Rams and Bengals. It will likely work for you as well.

Second, how often do great leaders become available? Rams head coach Sean McVay told NBC's Chris Simms prior to the game that they become available only on the rarest of occasions. Smart leaders know there is a difference between sensing opportunity and seizing it. That's why when future Hall of Famers Stafford, cornerback Jalen Ramsey, and defensive end Von Miller all became available, the Rams both sensed and seized the opportunity to secure the talents of each one.

Third, you can't overpay for great leaders. Great leaders pay for themselves. Notice this:

- The Rams traded their 2020 and 2021 first-round picks along with their 2021 fourth-round pick for Jalen Ramsey.

- The Rams traded their 2022 and 2023 first-round picks, a 2021 third-round pick, and quarterback Jared Goff for Matthew Stafford.

- The Rams traded their 2022 second- and third-round picks for Von Miller.

The NFL Draft is a three-day event. The first round is held on Thursday, rounds two and three on Friday, and rounds four through six on Saturday. With the exception of third-round compensatory pick guard Logan Bruss of Wisconsin selected at the 104th spot, the Rams had nothing to do for the first two days of the 2022 Draft.

First-round picks have traditionally been viewed as highly valuable assets. But would you trade some Draft Day inactivity and four first-round picks for a Super Bowl championship? Absolutely! Any day of the week and twice on Sunday! Whatever price the Rams paid for their trio of star players was worth it. The same goes for whatever price you would pay for the right leader.

Fourth, what separates good players from great players is the ability to execute under pressure. Big-time players make big-time plays in big-time games. Nowhere was this more apparent than in the Super Bowl's final two minutes. Matthew Stafford and wide receiver Cooper Kupp literally put the franchise on their shoulders and drove the team down the field for the winning touchdown. Then in the Bengals' final drive, the Rams' best player, defensive tackle Aaron Donald, made two plays which finished off the Bengals and secured the team's victory.

The Rams' three best players made big-time plays in the critical moments of the biggest game in the franchise's history. When your organization faces high-pressure situations, it is your top leaders who have the responsibility to lead your team through challenging times. It's why they are in leadership positions in the first place.

Fifth, we learned hard work and efficiency are greater than volume of activity. The game's unsung heroes were Duke Tobin, the Bengals director of football operations, and Steve Radicevic, their director of pro scouting. These team executives put together a championship-worthy defense. Seven of the team's eleven defensive starters were signed in the last two years as free agents.

In addition, the team drafted their best offensive players in the last two NFL Drafts—Burrow and wide receiver Ja'Marr Chase. The team also drafted wide receiver Tee Higgins, who caught two touchdown passes in the game, in the second round of the 2020 NFL Draft. Also, the Bengals drafted kicker Evan McPherson in the fifth round of the 2021 Draft. McPherson was the best kicker in football during that year's playoffs, as he successfully kicked all fourteen field goal attempts and six extra points. McPherson went 20-for-20 and scored forty-eight points during the Bengals' four play-off games. His 31-yard field goal in overtime against the Chiefs sent the Bengals to the Super Bowl.

What makes this level of talent acquisition even more impressive is the small size of the Bengals scouting staff. This is where efficiency comes in. The team, which has been accused of extreme frugality, only had eight staffers. No other NFL team had less than fifteen. In fact, seventeen teams have more than twenty. Division rivals Cleveland Browns have thirty and the Baltimore Ravens led the league with thirty-five.

What the Bengals scouting staff has done is simply astonishing. They have proven to all small businesses and organizations that if you are efficient, you can make up for the constraints placed upon you by lack of resources.

Finally, the difference between success and failure is tissue-paper thin. Just two seconds can literally change the legacies of countless people. A day after the game, a picture was released, showing Jalen Ramsey had fallen to the ground leaving Ja'Marr Chase *wide open* on the game's final play. But as previously mentioned, Aaron Donald sacked Bengals quarterback Joe Burrow to secure the Rams' victory.

But what if Burrow would have had just two more seconds to see the wide-open Chase and deliver him the ball? What if the Bengals' offensive line would have held their block on Donald for just two more seconds? Or what if Donald would have slipped, coming out of his stance? If any of these would have happened, Joe Burrow and Ja'Marr Chase would have gone down in NFL lore for having one of the most miraculous last-second victories in NFL history. It is possible Matthew Stafford would not make the Hall of Fame when his career is over. Jalen Ramsey would have been a heel rather than a hero. And rather than being the boy genius, Head Coach Sean McVay might well be considered as a coach who can't win the Big One after his second Super Bowl loss.

It is amazing what a difference two seconds can make in a leader's legacy. If you have elite training, breathtaking health, and are highly efficient, two seconds may be all you need to become mighty and go from pandemic to progress.

CHAPTER 1 STUDY AND DISCUSSION QUESTIONS

Do you consider yourself a productive person? What evidence would you supply to support your claim?

_____

_____

_____

In what areas of your life could you be more productive? What would be necessary for you to do so?

_____

_____

_____

What current training are you going through to become more productive as a leader? Why did you choose this particular plan? What results are you seeing?

_____

_____

_____

What are three things you need to edit from your life right now to become more productive and why?

_____

_____

_____

How is your health? What is one thing you can do today to become healthier and more productive? Is there anything preventing you from taking action right now?

_____

_____

_____

CHAPTER 2

Passion

And next to him among the three mighty men was Eleazar the son of Dodo, son of Ahohi. He was with David when they defied the Philistines who were gathered there for battle, and the men of Israel withdrew. He rose and struck down the Philistines until his hand was weary, and his hand clung to the sword. And the Lord brought about a great victory that day, and the men returned after him only to strip the slain.

—2 Samuel 2:9–10 (ESV)

The second of the Mighty Men we are introduced to is Eleazar. There are several things we learn from the passage above about this individual. He was a son and grandson. Eleazar was also a mighty warrior. In fact, he fought alongside David. But it is a battle they had with the Philistines where we learn our most important lessons about this particular Mighty Man. It is this lesson that if applied, will help you become mighty and go from pandemic to progress.

From Eleazar, we learn *passion*.

We often water-ski over certain biblical texts and don't take time to actually ponder what has been recorded for our benefit. Verse 10 contains only thirty-nine words but paints a more compelling picture than the opening scenes of *Gladiator* or *Saving Private Ryan*.

The text says, "the men of Israel withdrew." In other words, they retreated. We don't know why they retreated. Perhaps they were frightened and cowardly. Or maybe they were significantly outnumbered and in their "prudence" and "discernment" thought it was best to simply fight another day. Laziness, not wanting to put the work required to defeat the Philistines, was perhaps the issue. Maybe they didn't have the weaponry, the tools, or resources needed to be victorious. In any event, they left Eleazar out to dry, or so it seemed.

I love how verse 10 says, "He rose." Think of the drama. Here is a man all alone and facing a seemingly insurmountable challenge. I imagine Eleazar reaching down, tightening the laces on his sandals, rubbing dirt on his hands, and properly positioning his helmet and breastplate. And as this great warrior stood to his feet and faced his enemy, I can almost see him close his eyes and whisper a prayer to God for strength and protection.

As he opened his eyes, I think Eleazar reaches into the sheath attached to his belt and pulls out a sword but not just any sword. This sword has been with him in countless conflicts and been used when leading his troops to numerous victories. You can almost hear the music playing in the background! Despite having no support from his teammates and limited resources, Eleazar fought valiantly that day and experienced victory. But he likely paid a heavy price.

His hand became weary. Much like Josheb-basshebeth, he needed to be in tremendous physical condition and use an economy of motion. There could be no wasted energy. He simply did not have the margin. Eleazar would have been drained of all his physical strength, but he had the one thing he needed for victory, and the one of things you and I need for victory moving forward. He had passion.

"His hand clung to the sword." In other words, they literally had to pry the sword from his hand. I imagine this great warrior kneeling or lying on the ground, covered in sweat, dirt, and blood. Eleazor was probably surrounded by countless dead enemy soldiers he had slain during battle but likely did not come out of this battle unscathed himself. Eleazor would probably need medical attention and be scarred from this conflict. His face was likely covered in blood, and his body punctured from enemy spears and arrows. Once they got him up, I imagine Eleazor would need assistance getting off the battlefield because of dehydration. He could barely walk. *But his hand clung to the sword.*

Eleazor was so in the moment, so committed to victory, so about the task and assignment, that I imagine fellow soldiers coming up to him, reaching out their hand and saying, "Eleazor, it's over. You can let go of the sword now. Give me the sword. Eleazor; look at me! It's OK. Give me the sword." And then they pull the sword from his hands like you pry something from the jaws of a pit bull. That's passion.

I define passion as owning the result. Passionate people have an "over my dead body," "leave it all on the field," of "you've got to pry this sword from my hand" mentality. Chicago White Sox Scout Kevin Burrell teaches there are three levels of passion all leaders need to know about when assessing the level of ownership they and their teams have. I have added an additional level (Level 1) to Kevin's original list.

Level 1—You *Loathe* It
In other words, you hate your job or whatever you are involved in at the moment. It is simply a transactional relationship for you. They give you a certain amount of money, and you give them the minimum amount of time and effort required to make it an acceptable exchange. At this level, you are a prime candidate for quiet quitting. You are short-term at best.

Level 2—You *Like* It
You enjoy what you do and are actually pretty good at it. It meets your personal or financial needs, and better yet, your efforts are having

a positive impact in the lives of others. It gives you a reason to get out of bed in the morning. But if something better comes along, you will take it.

Level 3—You *Love* It

This is what most people think passion is. You love what you do and can't wait to get out of bed in the morning. You don't need an alarm clock. It's a great job or incredible endeavor you are involved in. You can't think of doing anything else. You are going to enjoy this as long as it lasts. This is an exciting place to be because many people never find this level of passion. You are beginning to live out your life's purpose and feeling a level of fulfillment you may have never experienced before.

Level 4—You *Live* It

This is what true passion is. You own the result of not just yourself but your entire organization as well. Your day does not end at 5:00 p.m. Continual improvement and ongoing education are your brand. You edit your life and have removed all the things preventing you from achieving your full potential. You're 24–7. You're all-in. This type of person is truly indispensable to your organization. They had to pry Eleazor's sword out of his hands. You will have to pry this type of person out of your organization. But why would you want to?

So ask yourself this question and to those on your team—Do you loathe it, like it, love it, or live it? The answer will determine your and their level of passion.

When it comes to living it, we are very aware of things like sexual misconduct, financial impropriety, and anger issues as disqualifiers for someone in leadership. However, there is another list of items, which can disqualify you from leadership and are rarely talked about.

Kevin is one of my favorite leaders and as fine a Christian man as you will ever meet. But don't let his kind demeanor fool you when it comes to evaluating talent. Kevin is also a man of extremely high standards.

He was evaluating a player described as "a top name for 2023." Yet, after watching him perform on a number of occasions, he classified him as "a work in progress" and will continue to monitor his progress over the next year.

After Kevin posted his evaluation on Twitter (omitting the player's name), I gleaned ten things which can disqualify you not only as a major league prospect, but from leadership as well. These are the issues Kevin identified:

1. Lack of passion. You don't love or live the game or your organization's mission or vision.

2. Lack of effort. This player did not run balls out and had poor body language. Effort is a decision and something you can control.

3. Not coachable. You have an ego problem and are not open to instruction.

4. Poor teammate. You are high-maintenance and bring others down.

5. Struggle to make in-game adjustments. You are rigid.

6. Immaturity. You are not mentally or emotionally ready for leadership.

7. Selfish. You want all of the attention.

8. Unbalanced. You lack the fundamentals to lead.

9. Poor attitude. Attitude is also a choice which determines your altitude. People with poor attitudes have a low leadership ceiling.

10. Undisciplined. As Kevin pointed out, the pain of discipline is always less than the pain of regret.

Just to reiterate, it is not often talked about, but having any of these ten issues can disqualify you from leadership. If anything on this list describes you, the time to make changes is now.

NEHEMIAH

One person who was the antithesis of the player Kevin scouted is Nehemiah from the Old Testament. Few leaders have ever lived their assignment as much as Nehemiah did. One of the many things this great leader did was casting a compelling vision of a brighter future.

Leaders with passion *love* casting vision! A vision is a gift solely given to the leader. The team doesn't get the vision; the leader does. As a result, a vision of a preferred future is so exciting that leaders can't wait to tell others about it and invite them to be part of it of this brighter tomorrow.

In Nehemiah 2:17, Nehemiah gives us a lesson on the proper sequence and timing when it comes to casting vision. He told the local officials, *"Then I said to them, 'You see the trouble we are in, how Jerusalem lies in ruins with its gates burned. Come, let us build the wall of Jerusalem, that we may no longer suffer derision.'"*

Notice the sequence—Nehemiah tells the people the trouble they are in and then invites them to head toward a more peaceful future. By communicating the problem prior to the solution, Nehemiah did the following:

- He educated the people by making them aware a problem existed.
- He then created buy-in from those who would benefit most from the solution to the problem.
- Finally, he created a sense of urgency that "this cannot continue. This problem must be fixed now."

Once the people were ready to solve the problem, it was then time to cast vision. Because of impatience and/or excitement, many leaders inadvertently make the mistake of inverting this process. They rush it. They are so excited about the vision, they immediately begin talking about this beautiful utopia of what could be. With great passion they describe this preferred future and promptly begin inviting people into it.

But something is missing from this approach. While the future is quite compelling, the sense of urgency for it hasn't been built up. As a result, it lacks complete buy-in and whole-hearted support from the people. The leader has microwaved their vision rather than crockpotting it. And we all know things taste better coming from a crockpot rather than a microwave.

Nehemiah gives leaders with passion a successful blueprint for vision-casting. After creating need and urgency, only then invite people to be part of the solution and go to a brighter tomorrow.

Nehemiah also gives a leadership clinic and five-step process into how to rally people around a compelling vision. In 4:19–20 he says, "The work is great and widely spread, and we are separated on the wall, far from one another. In the place where you hear the sound of the trumpet, rally to us there. Our God will fight for us." Notice these five steps:

1. Give a clear message. There is no lack of clarity in what Nehemiah is saying.
2. Define reality. "The work is great."

3. Eliminate isolation. Bring people together. "We are separated on the wall..."
4. Give the team a clear call to action. "Where you hear the sound of the trumpet, rally to us there."
5. Trust God for the victory. "Our God will fight for us." As we will learn later, there is no opportunity for victory apart from God's help.

SEBASTIAN STEUDTNER

Speaking of brighter tomorrows, passionate leaders have a keen sense of what they look like and take full advantage of them. They know it when they see it.

In October 2020, Austrian professional surfer Sebastian Steudtner was participating in an event off the coast of Nazaré, Portugal. He suddenly began to notice a large wave beginning to form behind him. But what was forming was not just any wave. In fact, it was going to be the wave of lifetime. It is in these moments when leaders are forced to make a life-altering decision. Will they have the passion needed to move from sensing opportunity to actually seizing it? Steudtner seized his opportunity and owned the result.

He instructed his Jet Ski driver Alemão Maresias, "Get me (to) this wave now." Maresias pulled him by rope to within approximately sixty yards of the swell. Steudtner then released the rope and approached the breaker. He said, "I'll never forget what I saw when I started to drop behind the peak and saw the entire wave."

Seizing this type of opportunity forced him out of his comfort zone to say the least. But this was a good thing. Being uncomfortable stretched and challenged him, just like it would any of us. He noted, "I started to accelerate like crazy. I had tears from the wind speed and was just holding on with everything I had—not doing anything funny, just hanging on." But at the edge of uncomfortable, the place where are you feel like you're just hanging on, is where greatness happens. By the time Steudtner had finished, he had surfed the largest wave ever recorded. He set a world record by riding a wall of water measuring eighty-six feet tall!

Seizing opportunity also allowed him to do something he never would have previously expected. Steudtner concluded, "Being from Germany and Austria, I wasn't meant to be a surfer. Anything that you can dream up and set your sight on, if you never give up and pursue it, you can reach it."

Passionately seizing opportunity allows you to have unforgettable experiences, achieve greatness, and do things you would never expect. Knowing this, why wouldn't you want to show the passion needed to own the result by seizing every opportunity which comes your way?

ANDREW WIGGINS

A similar chance to seize opportunity occurred in the Golden State Warriors 109–100 win in Game 3 of the Western Conference Finals against the Dallas Mavericks on May 22, 2022. With 6:39 remaining in the fourth quarter and the Warriors leading 91–83, Andrew Wiggins dribbled through the lane from the right wing before elevating over Luka Doncic for an emphatic dunk. It would become the signature play of the signature game of his entire career. Wiggins would finish with twenty-seven points and eleven rebounds.

Afterward, he said, "You know, some people never get the opportunities I have now, so you can't take this for granted." After not fulfilling the potential of a number one overall pick in the 2014 NBA Draft, a "lane opened up" for him literally and figuratively after being traded to

Golden State. Wiggins felt fortunate to have an opportunity to succeed. He did not take it for granted and took advantage of it.

Warriors head coach Steve Kerr said, "I think the way this series has mapped out, there's space for him to attack. You know, the way they are guarding Steph (Curry) and Klay (Thompson), the lineups that are out there for both seems there's some room for Wiggs to attack."

Leaders can take a lot from Kerr's comments—primarily, to seize opportunity, you need space. The obstacles which prevent you from personal, professional, and organizational success must be removed. For example, if red tape, antiquated policies and procedures, tradition, or unnecessary bureaucracy are preventing progress or accomplishment, it should be eradicated. The presence of Curry, who is often double-teamed, and Thompson have freed Wiggins up, and he has thrived with his newfound freedom.

Curry added, "It's amazing to see it happening under the bright lights. You don't know how guys are gonna respond when they're asked to do what we're asking them to do at this stage in the season, in the playoffs, when you have the highest hopes. But he's stepping up and that's only because of his approach and his attitude and just being a gamer." Curry's comments remind us that defining moments and catalytic events happen most often for those with a positive approach and attitude. As has been mentioned, a positive attitude is a great differentiator and creates chances to seize opportunities for those who have it.

To summarize, Andrew Wiggins's career-defining dunk teaches us that if you want to create and accelerate positive momentum for you and your organization, remove obstacles preventing freedom and success, have a positive attitude, and then seize your opportunity.

DILLON HELBIG

Let's go from experienced leaders on a public stage like Steudtner and Wiggins to a very young one with little to no fanfare. Let me introduce you to Dillon Helbig. At the time of this writing, Dillon is eight years old and has become an unexpected celebrity in the city of Boise, Idaho. Why? Dillon recently wrote an eighty-one-page Christmas book entitled *The Adventures of Dillon Helbig's Chrismis*. (This is not a misspelling.) The author is listed as Dillon His Self. Don't you just love eight-year-olds!

Dillon's book, which he also illustrated, is about Dillon being transported back to 1621 after his Christmas tree explodes. For the record, 1621 is when the first Thanksgiving holiday took place in the United States. Rather than going through the traditional publishing route, he merely went down to his local library and snuck his book onto a shelf. Talk about owning the result and bypassing the bureaucratic process!

Dillon said to a local television station, "There was a lot of librarians that I had to sneak past, so do you know what I did? I covered up this part and covered the back with my body and just snuck it in . . . I always be sneaky, like how I get chocolate." Alex Harman, the library's manager, said, "Dillon's book definitely fit all the criteria that we would look for to include a book in our collection." Therefore, they processed it accordingly and made the book part of their library's collection. Surprisingly, the book has gained significant traction. A waiting list as long as fifty-six people were in line to read Dillon's book.

Whether you lead a church, nonprofit, athletic organization, or business, there are several leadership lessons we learn from Dillon about passion.

First, leaders must deeply believe in their work. If you don't believe in your own work, why should anyone else? As previously mentioned,

Dillon "donated" his only copy of the book to the library. The only copy. His book was not going to be on the family bookshelf or coffee table. That's what I would do. In fact, I keep a number of my books in my personal possession. But not Dillon. He was all in.

Second, we learn greatness takes time and effort. Can you imagine the amount of work it would take for an eight-year-old to write and fully illustrate an eighty-one-page book? That level of focus and commitment for such an age is astonishing! Even as an eight-year-old, Dillon intuitively knew he had to pay a significant personal price to achieve his goal of writing a book.

Third, we are reminded of the value of creativity and its relationship to passion. You cannot have creativity without creation. Dillon creatively came up with a Christmas story he creatively illustrated. Creativity is also about solving problems. Dillon creatively thought of the public library as a means for distribution of his art. He then creatively snuck the book past the librarians and onto the shelf. The rest is creative history.

Finally, successful leaders like Dillon do not make excuses. They always find a way. Dillon was not going to be denied in his quest to get his book into as many hands as possible. His age was not going to be an excuse. Being a first-time author was not going to be an excuse. Neither was not having a well-known publisher, big budget, slick marketing campaign, or being in a major market. He had a dream to get his book into as many hands as possible, and he was going to make it happen, no matter what!

If an eight-year-old has the passion to achieve his goal of being an author, you and I are without excuse when it comes to achieving our goals. Do the work, pay the price, get creative, stop making excuses, and find a way to serve as many people as possible.

COACH PRIME, DEION SANDERS

One leader who has done all these things and is defined by passion is former Jackson State University and current Colorado Buffaloes head football coach Deion Sanders, known as Coach Prime. Coach Prime changed the culture of this Historic Black College and University's football program. During his three seasons as the JSU's head coach, Coach Prime amassed a 27–6 record, going 23–3 in his last twenty-six games.

One of Coach Prime's strengths is his superlative motivational and communication skills, which can be found in the following quotes on passion:

- "The one thing a coach really wants is to have is a team full of men who love the game."
- "Whatever you're giving is going to require sacrifice. What are you sacrificing?"
- "The sacrifice needs to be greater than the gift."
- "Ninety percent of you are not going pro whether you believe it or not... So I've got to prepare you for life. I've got to spend more time on the life part than the pro part."

But what resonated with me most in a YouTube video of Coach Prime speaking to his team was when he communicated what he needed each young man to do for the team to dominate that week's opponent. The players at JSU needed to be fully rested, prepared, consistent, knowing their job, and how to do it.

But Coach Prime didn't stop there. He also said they needed to eliminate distractions, have passion, purpose, and love—so much so, they needed to empty themselves on the field and have nothing left. He said, "I want you to leave with nothing left. I don't know how some of you can party after a game." If they could, they needed to reevaluate their effort and determine if they truly gave their best.

Sanders reminded me of University of Georgia Bulldogs head coach Kirby Smart telling their fans in an October 30, 2022 tweet prior to its November 5th game against the top-ranked Tennessee Volunteers, "If you can talk when you leave, you didn't yell enough." I guess the Bulldog Nation yelled enough. The Dawgs won 27–13. But back to Coach Prime.

Finally, Coach Prime advised the team they did not have to wait to the following weekend's game to do these things. They needed to start doing it today at the team's practice. Passionate leaders are always calling out the best in their teams and expecting them to go to the next level. Are you asking for the same level of commitment from those you lead?

CHRIS PAUL

Leaders with passion are natural collaborators because you can accomplish more with others than you can by yourself. They understand the value their teammates bring and work very hard to keep them engaged. But from time-to-time, circumstances dictate that the leader must get a little selfish and simply take over. If the organization is going to achieve its goal, the leader must own the result at a visceral level. It is one of those "over my dead body" type of situations.

Such a moment occurred during Game 1 of the Phoenix Suns–New Orleans Pelicans 2022 playoff series. The Suns all-star guard, Chris Paul, scored nineteen of his thirty points in the fourth quarter of the team's 110–99 victory. Head Coach Monty Williams told *The Athletic*, "That's just classic Chris. At the right time, he takes over, and we needed it."

From Coach Williams's comments, we learn three ways for leaders to know it is time to take over.

First, Paul had previously asserted himself at key moments multiple times throughout his Hall of Fame career. As Williams pointed out, this is "just classic Chris." Teammate Devin Booker added, "He's built for these moments." A leader should only take over when he or she has a track record of success when doing so. If not, continue to trust your teammates and others around you.

Second, leaders must intuitively know *when* it is time to take over. It takes a sixth sense. This is part of nuanced leadership often displayed by veteran leaders. The Pelicans had cut the Suns' lead to only eight points, 79–71, at the end of the third quarter. The Suns were becoming insecure and beginning to panic. Pressure was setting in. Momentum was on the side of the Pelicans. It was now time for Paul to step forward, and he did.

Finally, a leader should take over when their team needs them to. With the lead now in single digits and momentum beginning to shift to the Pelicans, Paul scored seventeen of the team's next nineteen points and assisted on the other two. *The Athletic's* Jason Quick observed that Paul seemed to be toying the Pelicans' defenders. The result of Paul stepping up was a Phoenix Suns victory.

As a leader with passion, if you are sensing your team needs you to assert yourself and you have done so in the past with great success, then it's likely time for you to take over once again.

WHEN THE MOMENT IS TOO BIG

Chris Paul stepped up when his leadership was required and owned the result. But what about other leaders who shrink from challenges?

What about leaders who are known for their passivity and lack of engagement? Not every leader owns the result at a visceral level. There are leaders who don't say, "Over my dead body." Rather, they say, "This is too much. I'm out."

I was recently speaking with a former pro football player who told an interesting story from his college-playing days. He said a hot-shot new quarterback ran into huddle during the team's first game. The coaches then signaled the play in from the sidelines. The ten other offensive players waited for the quarterback to call the play but were surprised to watch him just stare wide-eyed at everyone. This former player telling the story noticed the play clock was running down, but the quarterback was not saying anything. The hot-shot athlete was frozen by the moment. He was a "deer in headlights." Time was running out. Someone needed to step up and call the play.

The player I was speaking with was a senior at the time and knew the plays like the back of his hand. Therefore, he called the play himself. The team immediately lined up and ran the play successfully. For the rest of the game, he called every single play, rather than the quarterback. In fact, he called the plays for the rest of the season!

There are four important lessons any leader can take from this story. First, you can't own the result if you don't know the fundamentals of your profession. One of the possible reasons the quarterback froze was he did not know the team's plays as well as he should have. A lack of institutional knowledge will cause you to freeze and under-perform as a leader.

Second, some moments are simply too stressful for a leader. There are times when you see a leader freeze in uncomfortable situations. This may be because of a hard conversation, tense meeting, sales pitch with a high-profile prospect, or public speech. The lights are just too bright. These are times when the stress can be just too much for the leader.

Third, if you do not own the result, trust me, someone will always fill that leadership vacuum. Just like the player who started calling the plays, if you as the leader do not step up when leadership is required, someone or some group of people will step in and fill that void if, for no other reason, because this is what leaders do. They lead and solve problems.

Finally, smart leaders build a great team around them. This is part of owning the result. Leaders are not perfect. I'm not. Neither are you. In fact, even the best leaders have areas in their lives in which they are woefully sub-par. By having a skilled and competent team around you, they can fill in the gaps and support you in your areas of weakness. Nothing helps you own the result better than having a passionate team around you.

THE GRAND TETONS

In addition to the previous four items mentioned, something else which robs leaders of passion is exhaustion. You're just plain tired. Energy has been depleted. In the fall of 2022, my wife and I had the opportunity to spend a week in Jackson Hole, Wyoming, one of the most beautiful places on the planet. It was the trip of our lifetimes, but it did not start out that way due to exhaustion on my part.

Because of long lines in the security section of Jackson-Hartsfield Airport in Atlanta and an even longer first-leg of the trip with an extended layover in Salt Lake City, the trip took up much of the day. When we arrived in Jackson Hole, the plane landed on the tarmac. My wife is not used to traveling, so I was focused on getting our carry-ons and personal items off the plane. Then we waited for a short time in baggage claim before getting our rental car. I then had to find the car itself, get all the luggage loaded, connect the phone, and get the GPS setup. All travelers know this is standard operating procedure. I had no complaints at all, but I was tired.

The following morning we rose early to see the famous Teton National Park and the Grand Tetons. As we began driving along the vast open plains along Highway 191, I was overwhelmed with the beauty and majesty of this incredible mountain range. The Tetons are everything they are reported to be.

I then noticed some buildings off in the distance at the base of the mountains. I said to my wife, "That looks like a school. What a great place to learn." Then it looked more like a business park. But as we got about a half-mile further down the road, I saw something which brought me great embarrassment. It wasn't a school or business park but rather the *airport*—the same airport where we landed just the day before!

I then looked at my wife and with great exasperation said, "Do you mean to tell me our plane landed at the base of the Grand Tetons, and I didn't even know it? Are you kidding me?!" My embarrassment was only eclipsed by how distracted I was the day before.

It was then I was reminded of several negative effects exhaustion has on leaders and their ability to have the passion needed to effectively lead their teams:

First, exhaustion causes you to focus on maintenance, not advancement. I was so focused on just getting off the plane, getting to my car, and making it to my condominium that I missed why I was there in the first place.

Second, exhaustion causes you to miss the moment. It is called "a moment" because it is just that, a moment. It happens, and it's gone. It's a moment. The Grand Tetons are grand. They are hard to miss. But I missed the moment even though I was at the base of the mountain range. Exhaustion caused me to miss what was right in front (actually behind) of me.

Third, exhaustion causes you to minimize the journey you are on. If I would have enjoyed the journey rather than just getting out of the airport as expeditiously as possible, I would have taken in everything along the way, especially the Tetons.

Fourth, exhaustion results in significant opportunity costs. It limits your peripheral vision. Once again, you only have enough energy for your focus to be on what's in front of you, causing you to miss everything else around you. You do not have the energy to devote to anything except the immediate.

Fifth, let's face it, exhausted people need rest.

A comfortable bed + soft pillows + plenty of sleep = a better perspective

Every leader must, from time-to-time, come apart, or they will come apart.

Finally, exhaustion causes you to miss God. Psalm 18:1–3 says, "I love you, O Lord, my strength. The Lord is my rock and my fortress and my deliverer, my God, my rock, in whom I take refuge, my shield, and the horn of my salvation, my stronghold. I call upon the Lord, who is worthy to be praised, and I am saved from my enemies." As awe-inspiring as the Grand Tetons are, those rocks were created by my Rock. In fact, those rocks bow down to my Rock.

For me, I missed The Grand Tetons upon my arrival. For you, it might not be as grand as the Tetons, it could actually be something small but still very important. But be careful to make sure you don't miss things because you're exhausted. Don't miss the moment because that's all it is, a moment.

FLORENCE CHADWICK

In addition to exhaustion, foggy days can rob you of passion. Let me explain. Perhaps you are going through a very difficult season in your life right now. It could be a challenging job, relationship, health scare, financial crisis, or something related to your faith. Whatever it may be, you feel you are in over your head. Options seem limited. There is no light at the end of the tunnel, and if there is, it is a train headed right toward you. You are thinking about tapping out. Bailing on your responsibilities has become a viable option. At worst, hope is lost. At best, it is in short supply.

Some of you have things in your life you should quit, but others of you are just tired of the struggle. You just don't think you can go on with this situation one more day. You certainly don't feel mighty, and you are definitely not moving from pandemic to progress.

But before quitting, I want to encourage you to hang in there by telling the story of Florence Chadwick. Chadwick was a world-renowned long distance, open-water swimmer. She was the first American woman to swim the Straits of Gibraltar, the Bosporus, and the Dardanelles. Most notably, Chadwick was also the first woman to swim the famous English Channel in both directions. Impressively, both were in world record times.

The Catalina Islands are located twenty-six miles off the coast of Los Angeles, California. In 1952, Chadwick set out to swim this stretch of water. As is standard practice in these instances, Chadwick was accompanied by a number of boats whose job it was to look out for sharks, provide food and other supplies, and be there in the event of exhaustion or any medical issues. One of those in Chadwick's party was her mother.

Things seemed to be going fine fifteen hours into the swim when a thick fog bank settled in over the Catalina Channel. Chadwick became disoriented and began telling her mom she did not think she could finish the swim. Her mom attempted to encourage her, but after another mile, Chadwick asked to be pulled from the water. After getting settled into the boat, Chadwick soon learned she had quit just one mile from shore. The thick fog had prevented her from seeing that her goal was easily within her grasp and was soon to be achieved.

I sympathize with Chadwick. We are all susceptible to falling into a "fog" from time to time. This could be the result of a tense conversation, failure, technological mishap, health scare, missed expectations, financial challenge, or family issue. Each of these can cause us to have "foggy days."

Foggy days rob us of perspective and clarity. We can lose our sense of direction. This fog prevents us from seeing how close we are to actually accomplishing our goals and objectives. Foggy days distort reality and cause us fear, frustration, and uncertainty. Being in a fog can ultimately rob us of the opportunity to achieve our dreams. That is what happened to Florence Chadwick that day in 1952.

Dr. Tim Elmore in his May 20, 2022 "Leading The Next Generation Podcast" stated that developing clear targets and goals are often the solution to successfully coming through foggy seasons in our lives. Tim adds these goals should be SMART—Specific, Measurable, Attainable, Realistic, and Timely. SMART goals will provide the clarity and direction needed to guide you out of foggy times and safely to shore.

So did Chadwick ever fulfill her desire of swimming the Catalina Channel? Two months after her initial failed effort, she attempted the swim again. Ironically, a fog bank settled in again at the same fifteen-hour mark. Chadwick surely could have thought "Oh no, here we go again. It's just not meant to be." She had to be tempted to give up. I know I would have been. But this time she knew how close she was to shore. Chadwick persevered and finished swimming the Catalina

Channel. In fact, she would go on to swim the Channel two more times, once in 1953 in record time.

So if you are thinking of quitting something you are involved in because it's just become too hard, remember Florence Chadwick and be careful to reconsider your decision. You may be on the precipice of not only achieving your goal but doing so in record time.

BOB SALEM

It is always an extraordinary moment anytime someone breaks a world record. But not all records are the same. Some records are just downright extraordinary. I want to introduce you to Bob Salem of Colorado Springs, Colorado. Eleazor would like Bob.

At 9:00 a.m. MST on Saturday, July 9, 2022, Salem embarked on a most unique challenge. To celebrate the 150th birthday of the city of Manitou Springs, Colorado, Salem began pushing a peanut up Pikes Peak using only his nose. Yes, you read that right! Salem would wear something that can only be described as a CPAP machine with an attached spoon covering his face to push a peanut up the thirteen-mile mountain.

Believe it or not, this had been done at Pikes Peak three times before. The most recent was in 1963 by Ulysses Baxter. The entire record-breaking journey took approximately six days as Salem reached the top of mountain at sunrise on Friday, July 15. If you don't think this is a noteworthy physical achievement, try simply pushing a peanut up your driveway with your nose. You will be exhausted (as well as laughed at by all your neighbors). To push a peanut for thirteen miles up a mountain is an extraordinary feat!

But the obvious question is "Why?" Why would a grown man, who could accomplish any number of things with his life, pick this unusual task? The following are some of my proposed reasons why:

Bob described himself as "eccentrically challenged." Most leaders like a challenge. They willingly accept the challenge of building a great company, developing ground-breaking technology, inventing something life-changing, doing something that stretches them physically, or simply enjoy learning something new. But not everyone fits neatly into those types of boxes. There are some leaders out there like Bob Salem who are, well, eccentric. Maybe I'm describing you.

Another reason may be that leaders simply want to serve others. The only successful philosophy of leadership is servant leadership. Salem's efforts raised a significant amount of money for the local homeless community. Anything a leader does, up to and including pushing a peanut up a mountain with their nose, should be done for the good of others. Mighty leaders are servant leaders.

A third reason is leaders are always looking for opportunities to honor others. In fact, the best leaders build a culture of honor. In addition to serving the less-fortunate by raising money for charity, Salem was also celebrating the 150th anniversary of the city's founding. Smart leaders know you cannot move into the future without first touching the past.

I mentioned earlier Eleazor would like Bob Salem. Why? Whether it was Eleazor's sword or Salem's spoon, both men were so passionate and owned the result at such a deep level, you literally had to pry the tools of their trade off their bodies. That's passion.

However, there are times leaders do the opposite. During times when ownership of the results is required, they do not display great passion. They demonstrate a lack of it and go as far as passing the buck and blaming others. Such an event took place on November 20, 2022.

You see, there are a number of critical mistakes a leader cannot afford to make if they want to maintain their influence. Leaders cannot violate trust. They cannot misappropriate the organization's financial resources. Leaders cannot fail to build a quality team around them. Some leaders may even lack the courage to make hard decisions. But one of the mistakes a leader cannot afford to make is blaming others for their team's performance. They must own responsibility for the organization's results.

ZACH WILSON

In an earlier chapter, we discussed Greg Cosell's assessment of New York Jets quarterback Zach Wilson and how to improve his production. However, on Sunday, November 20, 2022 Wilson would have one of the worst days of his professional career. He completed only nine of twenty-two passes for a paltry seventy-seven yards against the New England Patriots. Even worse, many were embarrassingly under- or overthrown to wide-open receivers.

Afterward, in the postgame news conference, Wilson was asked, "As an offense, though, you were only able to score three points. The defense only gave up three points. Do you feel like you let the defense down?" To which Wilson answered in a deadpan fashion, "No."

It was the type of response, which could divide a locker room. Wilson's statement could be a catalyst for creating an internal offense-versus-the-defense culture. Silos could be formed. Walls could be built. Unity could be destroyed. Why?

Because when leaders don't take responsibility for the organization's performance, a blame game ensues. People will also not follow a leader who they do not feel has their back. Whether true or not, Wilson came off like a leader who was all about himself, not others. Smart leaders know when the team does well, you give the credit away. When the team performs poorly, the leaders take the blame.

Wilson's response *should have been* something along the lines of, "I'm the quarterback. I'm the on-field leader of this team. Whatever happens, happens on my watch. We all need to get better but first and foremost, I need to get better. Three points is not enough to win in this league. Did I let the defense down? Yes. I also let the offense, the coaches, our ownership, the Jets fanbase, and even myself down. Tomorrow, we will look at the film and learn from this game. We'll figure out where we can improve and get back to work. We're still in the play-off picture. There's a lot of football left to play. And I need to improve so we can finish the season strong."

That's what leaders do. They take responsibility for the entire organization. As the old saying goes, they don't point fingers; they pull the thumb. Improvement starts with the leader. But because Wilson did not give this type of answer, we will have to wait and see if he can truly finish his tenure with the Jets strong. We do know he was made inactive for the following game.

John Maxwell taught us that everything rises and falls with leadership. So when there is failure, it starts with the leader. I'm sure many people reminded Zach Wilson of this leadership truth after his press conference. Perhaps you need to be reminded of it as well.

As we begin to conclude this chapter on passion, I want to revisit Eleazar and those who were supposed to be alongside him in battle, the men of Israel. The text tells us they retreated during battle but "returned after him only to strip the slain." In other words, the men of Israel were not there during the battle but returned to claim their fair share of the spoils after Eleazar's victory.

To provide some context, the spoils of victory were how soldiers were compensated during ancient times. After conquering the enemy, they would take their gold, silver, treasure, livestock, spices, and fine linens as form of payment. The victorious combatants would often leave nothing of value behind.

Even average leaders can read this account and become angry. They think, "Wait! They left when it got hard and came back only to get the benefit of the hard work of others!" And they would be right. I call these particular men of Israel "Photo-Op People."

Recently, I watched something happen, which caused me to have a certain level of anger as well. The source of my anger I have seen played out time-and-time again. It just gets frustrating after a while.

Several people were working very hard on a project, which would benefit hundreds of under-resourced people. Once all the hard work had been completed, a department leader showed up, and just moments later the CEO arrived as well. Guess who received all the credit from the CEO? You guessed it, the department leader who did none of the heavy lifting.

Even worse, not only did the department leader not credit the team with project's success, this person received the public praise from the event's organizers and took part in a photo-op with various community leaders. Guess who was not in the photo? The team who did all the work, that's who.

This is not an uncommon occurrence. It happens in countless organizations every single day. Few things are as disheartening and cause disillusionment as much as photo-op leaders. We don't need photo-op leaders; we need passionate leaders like Eleazar—passionate leaders who own the result, regardless of the cost.

How do you know the difference? The following are eight differences between Passionate People and Photo-Op People:

1. Passionate People are givers. Photo-Op People are takers.

2. Passionate People are about others. Photo-Op People are about themselves.

3. Passionate People arrive early and stay late. Photo-Op People arrive late and leave early.

4. Passionate People are about results. Photo-Op People continually tell you about their resume.

5. Passionate People are about paying whatever price is needed for success. Photo-Op People are about doing the least amount of work possible.

6. Passionate People seek out what is hard. Photo-Op People run from what is hard and seek out the path of least resistance.

7. Passionate People are about transformation. They are about changing lives. Photo-Op People are transaction. They are about what they can get out of the exchange.

8. Passionate People are about the big picture. Photo-Op People are about having their picture taken.

Leaders, next time a photo-op takes place, take a moment and figure out who did all the work and should be in the picture. This will allow you to give credit where credit is due and create a culture people want to be a part of. Make sure it is the people with passion—the people who owned the result—who are showcased.

CHAPTER 2 STUDY AND DISCUSSION QUESTIONS

Why is being passive so easy for leaders, and what results from it?

_____

_____

_____

Sebastian Steudtner surfed the largest wave recorded in human history. What large waves are you riding right now, and how does it make you feel?

_____

_____

_____

On a scale of 1–10, how exhausted are you as a leader? What is the source of that exhaustion? What changes are you willing to make so you can become refreshed and seize the opportunities available to you?

_____

_____

_____

When do you know it is the time for you to step up as a leader and own the result?

_____

_____

_____

When your organization has significant victories, would those around you describe you as a Passion Person or Photo-Op person, and what evidence would they give?

_____

_____

_____

CHAPTER 3

Resilience

> *"And next to him was Shammah, the son of Agee the Hararite. The Philistines gathered together at Lehi, where there was a plot of ground full of lentils, and the men fled from the Philistines. But he took his stand in the midst of the plot and defended it and struck down the Philistines, and the Lord worked a great victory."*
>
> —2 Samuel 2:11–12 (ESV)

We first met Josheb-basshebeth and learned about the value of production if you want to become mighty and move from pandemic to progress. Next, we met Eleazar. From this great warrior, we learned about the importance of passion, owning the result. Now we meet Shammah, and from him, we will learn about the value of resilience.

Just like Eleazar, we are told Shammah is a son. This is an important sidenote for leaders. Everyone you meet is someone's son or daughter. Therefore, each person should be treated with intrinsic value if for no other reason than that is how you would like for someone to treat your son or daughter.

But we also learned a group of Philistines had gathered at Lehi. Lehi was a strategic plot of land because it contained vast amounts of lentils. Lentils were an important part of the diet during this time in history. Earlier in 2 Samuel 17:27–29, it tells us, "When David came to Mahanaim, Shobi the son of Nahash from Rabbah of the Ammonites, and Machir the son of Ammiel from Lo-debar, and Barzillai the Gileadite from Rogelim, brought beds, basins, and earthen vessels, wheat, barley, flour, parched grain, beans *and lentils* (emphasis mine), honey and curds and sheep and cheese from the herd, for David and the people with him to eat, for they said, 'The people are hungry and weary and thirsty in the wilderness'." Lentils were a crucial component for hunger and strength to those traveling with David in the wilderness. So much so, they were willing to go to battle over it.

But once again, "the men fled the Philistines," leaving Shammah alone, much like Eleazar was. We will address it in the next chapter, but thirty-seven brave souls were identified as David's Mighty Men. However, we know from earlier, there were 400 men total with David in the wilderness. Therefore, I suspect the number of those who often fled during times of battle numbered in the hundreds.

Nonetheless, Shammah "took his stand in the midst of the plot and defended it and struck down the Philistines." While everyone else quit, Shammah stood his ground, fought with limited help and resources, and still prevailed. When the average person is fleeing but you stand firm and engage the issue, that's resilience. If you are going to become mighty and move from pandemic to progress, there will come times when you must be willing to stand alone.

When you read the Bible from Genesis to Revelation, all sixty-six books, you will discover God never called anyone to an easy task. If I could sit down over a cup of coffee and have a conversation with everyone reading this book, I would discover each of you have faced many challenging, often debilitating times in your life. Hard times, uncertainty, heartbreak, disappointment, and pain are all part of the small print of the leadership contract. They are constant companions. As a result, resilience is something every leader must develop.

But something very special happens when we persevere through challenging situations. These hard times force us to press into God. Oftentimes, we have to drop to our knees and completely rely on God and God alone. We learn the foundation of our resilience is found in our reliance on God, the one who loves to be depended on, to be strong in areas of weakness.

Dr. Crawford Loritts in his masterful book, *Leadership as an Identity: The Four Traits of Those Who Wield Lasting Leadership*, writes:

> But it is this wonderful sense of helpless inadequacy that keeps me running to our loving, gracious, and, yes, merciful heavenly Father for His strength. I have learned that He loves to hear me say, "Father, I can't do what You have called me to do without You. In fact, I can't make it without You. If You don't come through, It's all over. Please, Father, do Your work through me!" And time and again I can hear Him whispering those sweet words, "Crawford, you are where I want you to be. Place all that is before you in My hand, trust Me and I will accomplish through you what I have called you to do."

While not a theologian like Dr. Loritts but still a very smart man, Henry David Thoreau once wrote, "What lies behind us and what lies ahead of us are tiny matters compared to what lies within us."

Someone with a lot inside of them is Carey Lohrenz. Carey is a former lieutenant in the United States Navy. She is famous for becoming the first female fighter pilot of the F-14 Tomcat. She writes in her book *Fearless Leadership: High-Performance Lessons From The Flight Deck*, "Resilience is what you'll need to call upon when you face a major, life-changing circumstance, one you probably didn't see coming and probably didn't cause through any action of your own. Resilience is what you need when everything blows up in your face—when it feels as though you were just hit by a meteor."

TWO TYPES OF STORMS

When it feels as if everything has blown up in your face and you have just been hit by a meteor, you need to know how to properly evaluate the situation. To help in this area, we will use another example from nature—storms. Storms in our lives are not just weather-related, they can take on many forms. As previously mentioned, it can be a bad report from our doctor, an unexpected job loss, financial crisis, family dysfunction, or devastating tragedy. During these times, we feel heavy winds blowing, flood waters rising, walls crashing in, and our foundation being shaken. We have all been there. Some reading this book are there right now. It's been said we're either in a storm, coming out of a storm, or going into one.

I used to think life was a series of good times with occasional storms along the way. I have come to believe life is a series of storms with occasional good times along the way. But there are two types of storms we go through in our lives. There are storms of correction and storms of perfection. And they are very different.

Storms of correction are of our own doing. They are the consequences of bad decisions. We may have financial hardship because of going into debt or making unnecessary purchases. Perhaps you have lost influence in your organization because of reckless behavior. I know many parents who, in their later years, have no relationship with their children. This is because of anger and abusive behavior during their upbringing. On a personal note, I wrote earlier about my Type 2 adult-onset diabetes. This health storm is my own fault because of a decades-long unhealthy love of sweets and carbohydrates. I could have blamed my parents, advertisers, or culture, but the fact is there was no one to blame but myself. No one made me drink all that sweet tea and eat all those cookies and doughnuts. I just loved the taste of sweets, but it came with the serious consequences I am now experiencing. These are storms of correction. What's worse, those who you love are often victims from the shrapnel of your poor decisions.

Then there are storms of perfection. This is when life just happens. You may be doing an excellent job, but the home office in another state decides to shut down your division. There are many people who just happen to live in an area which experiences a natural disaster. Many of us know people who were in perfect health and passed away unexpectedly. What about when you are not at fault in a car accident? There are also countless good parents whose children simply made bad decisions. Someone else's storm of correction often turns into your storm of perfection. Storms in our lives force us into a time of self-reflection and reflecting on God Himself.

GREAT QUESTIONS

Many families have a door, door frame, or area in their home where they measure the height of their children or grandchildren each year on their birthday. For my family, it was a tree located in my grandparents' backyard. This year-to-year comparison in height is a measurement of physical maturity.

So how do you measure mental and emotional maturity in your children? When my daughter Anna was three years old, we took her to Grant Park Zoo in Atlanta. I said, "Anna, if you could ask me any question in the world, what would it be?" She said, "Daddy, why do elephants stink?" This is a reasonable question from a three-year-old. One year later, we returned to the zoo for her fourth birthday, and I asked the same question. Anna asked if my stepfather who had died earlier in the year was in heaven. Anna's question revealed how much she had matured during the previous year.

Mental and emotional maturity are measured by the questions your children are asking. You can also learn a lot about the maturity of the leaders in your organization by the questions they are asking. For instance, if the questions from your leaders are about why type of paper you are using in the copier rather than what type of culture you are building, you are probably in trouble as an organization.

Mike Linch, the incomparable senior pastor of NorthStar Church in Kennesaw, Georgia, talked about three questions people ask when challenging times arise in their lives. The first question is "Why?" We all from time-to-time ask the "Why" question, but you don't want to stay in the "Why" phase very long. It is acceptable to date "Why," but you don't want to marry it. "Why" usually leads leaders to wrong decisions. There are two better questions to ask.

The second question is "What now?" Where continually asking "Why" will lead you to wrong decisions, asking "What now" will usually lead you in the right direction. Asking this question changes your focus. "What now" involves others. You may not be able to change what happened to you as a leader, but you can use your past issues to empathize and sympathize with others. Asking "What now" means your pain and disappointment will not be wasted. As Robin Roberts is credited with saying, "Make your mess your message."

The third question to ask is "How?" This question reveals your resilience and maturity as a leader. What you are saying is, "Lord, I don't know why this happened. I don't know how you are going to use it, but I trust you." As Mike pointed out, "Trusting God with 'how' always leads to peace and repentance." Mature leaders don't worry about the "How." That sounds counter-intuitive, but mature leaders have learned to leave the "How" to God.

Leaders, are you or your teams dealing with some challenging issues right now? If so, what questions are being asked, and what are those challenges revealing about your personal and organizational maturity?

STETSON BENNETT IV

Someone who had to have asked a lot of questions over the last few years is University of Georgia Bulldogs quarterback Stetson Bennett IV. On January 10, 2022 the Bulldogs defeated the Alabama Crimson Tide 33–18 to win the NCAA football championship. The game's iconic moment was Bennett's emotional reaction to the victory. Bennett was openly weeping on the sideline during the game's final moments. This outpouring of emotion and the story behind it teaches leaders many things.

First is the power of vision. We previously wrote on the subject of vision, but you know a vision for your life or organization is real when you don't have the vision, but the vision has you. Bennett's father often tells the story of his three-year-old son saying he wanted to grow up and play quarterback at the University of Georgia. It was this clear and compelling vision for his life that carried Bennett from a lightly recruited prospect to a two-time national champion and Heisman Trophy finalist.

Second, great talent often goes unrecognized. If you feel invisible to those around you and that your contributions are being overlooked and don't matter, Stetson Bennett IV should be an inspiration. Bennett led Pierce County High School in Blackshear, Georgia, to three consecutive state playoff appearances. In his senior year alone, he threw for 3,724 yards, ran for approximately 500 yards, and scored forty total touchdowns. Yet, the two-star prospect did not receive a single scholarship offer from a SEC school.

However, Bennett still had a burning desire to play quarterback for the Georgia Bulldogs. It was something he felt he must do and would go to any lengths to make his dream become reality. Bennett took the next step and walked onto the team as a nonscholarship player in 2017.

Third is the power of persistence. Buried on the team's depth chart, Bennett left after one year to play for the Jones College Bobcats, a junior college in Ellisville, Mississippi. While there, he led the team to a 10–2 record, the MACJC championship game and a Mississippi Bowl win over Eastern Arizona. Bennett passed for 1,840 yards (twelfth in the NJCAA) and sixteen touchdowns.

Even after a successful junior college season, Bennett was still rated a two-star prospect, according to 247Sports. The following was his recruiting profile written by Charles Power:

> Shorter quarterback who is listed under 6-feet. Has a naturally thin frame and has added some weight over the last few years and is likely maxed out in terms of manageable bulk ... Lacks stature and has average arm strength. Was not super productive in junior college with a high interception rate and low yards per attempt. Projects as a backup quarterback who will provide depth at the Power 5 level.

That doesn't sound like the recruiting profile of a quarterback who could lead a team to the national championship does it?

Fourth is the power of preparation. Bennett returned to the Dogs as a scholarship player in 2019. The following season, he was ranked third on the team's depth chart but kept working hard in case his chance to play ever came. Unexpectedly, the team's projected starter opted out, and then the backup struggled. But because of his preparation, Bennett was ready to play. He subsequently started half the team's games. This leads to the final point.

Finally, we learn the power of resilience. As the 2021 season approached, adversity remained a constant companion in Bennett's life. Transfer JT Daniels appeared to be the fans', media's, and coaches' favorite, heading into the season. Bennett only received twenty reps in the spring and fall practices combined. He considered transferring but chose to keep working hard and wait for his opportunity.

Opportunity finally presented itself, and Bennett seized it. Once he got into the lineup full-time, Head Coach Kirby Smart simply could not take him out. Throughout the season, even when doubted by his coach, staff, and UGA fanbase, Bennett never wavered in his confidence or his abilities. He just kept working hard, kept believing, and the team kept winning. The result today is two national championships.

There is an old Japanese philosophy which states if you cry in practice, you laugh in competition. Too many people quit way too early. In fact, as a society we have institutionalized quitting and sometimes celebrate it as "bravery." But as Coach Paul Assaiante, seventeen-time national champion in Men's Squash at Trinity College, said in a December 24, 2022, interview with *The Daily Coach*, "A sword is made strong by putting it through fire. . . . I try to create that sword." Regardless of how many obstacles and doubters Stetson Bennet IV faced, he never quit. And you shouldn't either. Become a strong sword.

ANTARCTICA

Stetson Bennett IV is a story about man versus man and man versus himself. Now let's discuss the importance of resilience when it comes to man versus nature.

Antarctica is the most uninhabitable place on Earth. Resilience is a prerequisite for even visiting there. And yet, eleven babies have been born there. The questions are why, and what does it mean for leaders?

Two countries, Chile and Argentina, wanted the rights to the land. Argentina dispatched (and yes, I specifically chose that word) a woman who was seven months pregnant to the continent. On January 7, 1978, this lady, who also happened to be married to a military official, gave birth to Emilio Marcos Palma. As a result of having the first natural-born citizen in Antarctica, Argentina felt they had rights to the land.

Not to be outdone, Chile later sent a young couple to the island to both conceive and give birth to a newborn baby. On November 21, 1984, Juan Pablo Camacho Martino was born. Chile now felt their claim on the land was more solid. Both countries continued to have babies in Antarctica, eleven in all. Interestingly, all eleven have survived, giving Antarctica the lowest infant mortality rate in the world. The following are the leadership lessons we learn from this unusual story:

First, it sounds basic, but leaders go first. Leaders are always breaking new ground. They go places no one else has gone before. John Maxwell has often said, "A leader knows the way, goes the way, and shows the way." So when no one had rights to this continent's land, a leader was going to figure out how to acquire them.

Second, smart leaders see great value in things others often overlook. The average person would look at Antarctica and see nothing but snow and ice. *Only penguins would enjoy this place*, they would think. But much like how America and Russia battled over space, Chile and Argentina saw strategic value where no one else did.

Third, leaders must also be willing to pay a price which others are unwilling to pay. Let's take a moment and think about the young men and women willing to give birth in Antarctica and the price they had to pay. I would imagine the birthing centers and care units were not up to the standards of the local hospitals they left behind. The weather is certainly not optimum for raising a young family. But for the good of their countries, they willingly made the sacrifice. That leads to my final point.

Finally, leaders sacrifice a lot for the good of their organizations. They work longer hours, sometimes go without paychecks, have hard conversations, and carry a level of stress no one can understand unless they are in a leadership position. But they pay that price because they are leaders, and that's what leaders do.

So which country, Chile or Argentina, owns the rights to Antarctica? Well, neither. It is still governed by a group of international countries who signed The Antarctic Treaty on December 1, 1959. It is land set aside for peace and science.

TSUNAMI SURVIVOR LISALA FOLAU

There is no dispute however on which country owns the island of Atata. It is one of the 171 islands known as Tonga. At approximately 7:00 p.m. on Saturday, January 15, 2022, a wave of over six meters high hit Atata's shore. This was the result of Hunga Tonga-Hunga Ha'apai volcano erupting underwater off the coast. The force of the eruption was more than 500 times that of the Hiroshima bomb dropped in World War II.

Lisala Folau was a fifty-seven-year-old retired carpenter and one of the sixty people populating the minuscule island. He was also disabled and had trouble walking. Folau was at his home, painting when the wave hit land destroying numerous homes. Despite seeking refuge by climbing a tree, Folau was swept out to sea.

Mr. Folau could hear his son calling his name, but he did not respond for fear of putting his son in danger. He said, "The truth is, no son can abandon his father. But for me, as a father, I kept my silence for if I answered him, he would jump in and try to rescue me. He would come, and we would both suffer."

Miraculously, Mr. Folau would eventually safely swim 4.7 miles to the main island of Tongatapu. He arrived at 10:00 p.m. the following day, twenty-seven hours after being initially swept out to sea. His story went viral, and online readers referred to him as "a legend" and "Aquaman." This is what the real-life "Aquaman" Lisala Folau (sorry Jason Momoa) teaches us about leadership and life:

First, life can change in an instant. Mr. Folau was enjoying a quiet evening, painting, when a tsunami suddenly hit his island home. Many of us can tell stories of just going about our everyday lives, just painting if you will, when suddenly disaster hit. Maybe it was a phone call, driving through an intersection, your supervisor asking if you could come into the office, or a routine doctor's visit. In any event, instantly our lives were changed forever.

Second, be resilient. That is what this chapter is about. Do not panic during troubling times. Being swept out to sea would definitely be a cause for panic to say the very least. Most of us, me included, would begin screaming and fighting for our lives. But Mr. Folau remained calm as he heard his son calling out for him. Astonishingly, he had the presence of mind to realize responding would only put his son in danger as well. Not only did remaining calm help save Mr. Folau's life, it likely saved his son's as well.

Third, focus on what you can do, not what you can't do. While Mr. Folau was disabled, but he was not helpless. There were things he could still do. He said, "I can't walk properly, both my legs are not working properly, and when I can, I believe a baby can walk faster than I. So I just floated, bashed around by the big waves that kept coming." Mr. Folau should inspire someone reading this page to not give up. Keep fighting. Keep floating. You're going to find land soon enough.

Fourth, resilient leaders are mentally tough and continually put their families first. He added, "It stayed with my mind if I can cling to a tree or anything and if anything happens and I lose my life, searchers may find me and my family can view my dead body." Leaders are often told that at the end of their lives, they will not be thinking about market performance, spreadsheets, taxes, or some other work-related item. They will be thinking about their families. Mr. Folau sure did.

Fifth, resilient leaders utilize the resources they have available to them. All Mr. Folau had at his disposal was a tree to hold onto, the ability to swim and float, and the will to live. This would not appear to be much, but it was enough for him to make it safely to the main island. When hard times hit, inventory the resources you do have at your disposal and utilize those to their fullest extent. Creative solutions flow from scarcity, not abundance.

Finally, difficult times will make us resilient or resentful. They will make us hateful or grateful, bitter or better. Mr. Folau chose the latter. At a press conference, he thanked God, his family, and his church for giving him the strength to survive. May the difficult times we face always remind us of God's goodness, protection, and provision as well.

REAL MADRID

Winston Churchill once said, "Success is not final, failure is not fatal: it is the courage to continue that counts." Successful and resilient leaders have learned that failure is not only a constant companion, but success ultimately comes from learning how to move forward and leverage failure.

On May 28, 2022, Real Madrid defeated Liverpool in soccer's Champions League Final 1–0. Afterwards, the two teams participated in one of the great traditions in all of sports.

At the match's conclusion, the winning team's players, in this case Real Madrid, formed an aisle toward the trophy stand. The losing team, in this case Liverpool, then walked through the aisle of winning players where they would then accept their runner-up medals. Afterward, Real Madrid made their way to the stand and accepted their trophy. This is an extraordinary demonstration of humility, grace, and sportsmanship as not everyone gets a trophy in Premier League, Champions League, and World Cup soccer. There are several lessons all leaders can learn from this moment about resilience and how to best handle failure.

The higher up you go, the more painful failure will become. Liverpool's incomparable manager Jurgen Klopp said earlier in the year, "If you want to win big, you have to be ready to lose big." He previously said, "The higher you climb performance-wise, the more likely it gets you'll have a stressful conclusion of the season." Baseball has a saying: swing big, miss big. Hopeless romantics often point out it is better to have loved and lost, than to have never loved at all. Leaders understand it is those who attempt to rise to the highest levels of their professions that often experience the greatest failure. But this is the leadership journey. It requires resilience, and we wouldn't have it any other way.

Leaders always go first, even in failure. The first person to walk through the second-place procession was Klopp. Shortly afterward came team captain Jordan Henderson. Their attitude and professionalism set the tone for their entire club. When your organization experiences failure or disappointment (and it will), your leaders must be resilient and maintain a positive attitude. The entire organization will take its cue from them. Klopp provided a perfect example on how to handle a loss.

Leaders should always show class and humility, especially in failure. I can only speak for myself. If I gave all I had for an entire year to win a championship, something I've dreamed of and prepared for my entire life, and then came up one goal short, it would be very difficult to walk past the opposition and congratulate every member of the team who just defeated me. My feelings of disappointment would just be too raw. But that is what the Liverpool players did. Their class and humility eclipsed their personal feelings. This is the perfect model for us to follow as leaders when we experience failure.

COACH TRENT DILFER

Another of my favorite leaders is Trent Dilfer. While coaching the Lipscomb Academy football team in 2019, the team lost to its archrival Christ Presbyterian Academy Lions 28–7. As shown in the documentary *Set Apart,* Coach Dilfer told his team in the post-game locker room speech, "I love y'all too . . . We just keep getting better, keep getting better. We'll be just fine. Do not flinch. Do not flinch. Come to work Sunday. Get better." And that is just what the team did.

The two teams would meet again later in the season but this time for the state championship. With Lipscomb trailing 10–0 at halftime, Dilfer enthusiastically addressed his team. He said, "I love this. I love how hard this is. I'm literally giggling inside. We have zero first downs on offense, our defense has been on the field seventeen minutes, given up 244 yards, we've missed multiple tackles, our quarterback is not playing good, we're slipping. You know what that is? That's hard stuff. That's exactly what I promised you this would be! So instead of being shell-shocked say, 'It's only ten-nothing.' We can score ten points like that!"

Keep getting better. Don't flinch. Love things which are hard. Giggle on the inside when things are hard. That's resilience.

Leaders should go even further than showing class and humility in defeat. They should rejoice with those who rejoice. Romans 12:15 says, "Rejoice with those who rejoice, weep with those who weep." As leaders, especially Christian leaders, we do a great job of weeping with those who weep. But we often do a terrible job of rejoicing with those who rejoice. Perhaps it is because we are envious and jealous. In contrast though, the Liverpool players and Coach Dilfer graciously congratulated their rivals in defeat. Which leads to the next point: leaders have rivals, not competitors. The Liverpool and Lipscomb players left it all on the field. In a competitive environment, all leaders should do likewise. Afterwards, if you lose, you should be resilient enough to graciously shake the hand of your rival and thank them because they are making you better.

One of the most important lessons a leader can take from failure is it is just a data point to learn from. Klopp once said, "The only reason for a defeat is to learn from it. If you learn from it, it's just a result. If you don't learn from it, it's a disaster." He added, "I didn't suffer too much after we lost. I suffered, but I just took it as information, and it's just more information which we all use to carry on." Within twenty-four hours after losing to Real Madrid, Klopp was already talking about the team's goals for 2023. The Liverpool soccer team was already learning from this defeat and planning to come back stronger the next year.

JAYSON TATUM

In contrast to Liverpool and Lipscomb, runners-up for their respective championships, let's look at the 2022 NBA runner-up Boston Celtics and comments made by the team's superstar Jayson Tatum. We have all seen leaders quit when things got tough. Sometimes we on the outside were blindsided by their decision, but we did not have to be. There were likely tell-tell signs the leader was giving us as warnings he or she was thinking about quitting.

On June 10, 2022, the Golden State Warriors defeated the Boston Celtics on their home court by the score of 107–97 in Game 4 of the NBA Championship Series. During the postgame news conference, Celtics star Jayson Tatum made a passing statement which many people did not notice, but discerning leaders were alarmed by. Tatum said, "It's a new series, best of three. Get some sleep and get on this long-#%@ flight tomorrow."

Only two wins away from winning his first NBA championship, Tatum was complaining about the length of the flight to California. Granted, a flight from Boston to San Francisco is a long one but a small price to pay for the opportunity to take significant steps toward becoming a NBA champion.

When leaders complain about the price that must be paid to lead, it is an indicator they may soon be no longer willing to pay that price. Everyone loves the perks of leadership. They love the spotlight, notoriety, compensation, expense accounts, corner office, and so forth. But few are willing to pay the price needed to lead. Complaining about the price of leadership is a sign a leader may soon be no longer willing to pay it.

Interestingly, the more successful you become, the greater the price you have to continually pay. Progress and pain have a comparative relationship. Jayson Tatum is an all-star and the team's best player. He was named the Most Valuable Player of the Eastern Conference Championship Series. Yet, Tatum was now complaining about a long flight, on a chartered jet, mind you, required to become a champion. Hopefully, someone in the Celtics organization reminded Tatum about his responsibility as the team's leader and how everyone would follow his example.

On the other hand, you know who did not complain about the length of the flight? Steph Curry did not complain about the flight. Neither did Klay Thompson, Draymond Green, Andrew Wiggins, or any of the other Warriors players. These experienced leaders all know a long flight is a small price to pay to become a champion.

If a leader in your organization shows a lack of resilience and has begun complaining about the price they are having to pay, kindly give them some perspective and remind them of the cost of leadership. Hopefully, they will respond accordingly. If not, make sure you have a healthy leadership pipeline because they may be soon quitting.

For the record, the Celtics lost the next two games.

Tatum's comments reveal a disturbing trend in many next-generation leaders. Many young leaders think their life and career will get "easier" when they make it to a certain leadership position. They also think it will be easier if they have the right team, better financial resources, a job in the right office or part of the country, first-class accommodations, or the perfect mentor or boss. What they soon find out is leadership never gets easier. For that matter, life doesn't either.

What experienced leaders have learned is that with ever new level in your life or career comes a new devil. Leadership never gets easier. What must change is not the challenge of the assignment, but the character and resilience of the leader undertaking the assignment.

COACH KARA LAWSON

Duke Blue Devils women's basketball coach Kara Lawson addressed this very issue with a group of players. The video of her speech went viral. Coach Lawson said with great conviction, "We all wait in life for things to get easier ... It never gets easier. What happens is you become someone who handles hard stuff better. So that's a mental shift that has to occur in your brains."

She continued, "And the second we see you handling stuff, handling hard better, what are we going to do? We're going to make it harder.

We're going to make it harder because we're preparing you for when you leave here."

Much like coaches Deion Sanders and Trent Dilfer who were preparing their players for life, so was Coach Lawson. Life is not easy. It puts up a fight. Therefore, she implored her players, "So make yourself a person who handles hard well. Not someone who's waiting for the easy . . . Because if you have a meaningful pursuit in life, any meaningful pursuit in life if you want to be successful, it's going to the people that handle hard well. Those are the people who get the stuff they want."

After delivering such a counter-cultural message, she began giving encouragement along with the hard dose of realism. Coach Lawson concluded, "Don't get discouraged through this time if it's hard. Don't get discouraged. It's supposed to be, and don't wait for it to be easy . . . So make yourself someone who handles hard well, and then whatever comes to you, you're going to be great."

So if you are going through something hard as a leader, rejoice. Get excited! You are probably on the right track. As Coach Lawson said, it's not supposed to be easy. It's supposed to be hard. Hard things create resilience, which is a must if you want to become mighty and move from pandemic to progress.

Chicago White Sox scout Kevin Burrell told me another story of scouting a major league prospect at a Power 5 school. The player struck out a critical point in the game. As he returned to the dugout, Kevin watched him walk past all the players to the Gatorade cooler.

At this point, I was expecting to hear a cautionary tale about the player kicking over the bucket or even smashing it with a bat. But that is not what happened. The player got two cups of Gatorade, one for himself and the other one he gave to the team's pitcher. Upon seeing this, Kevin smiled and said, "He gets it."

When this player experienced failure, he did not sulk or have a bad attitude. He did not have an outburst of anger. Rather, he served a teammate. When a leader experiences failure, first they should evaluate what happened and see what they can learn from it. Second, they should take those learnings and serve someone else. Serving others takes the focus off you and places it onto another person. It shows you are resilient and see the big picture. It shows that you know life is not about you.

Successful leaders ask two great questions, "So what? Now what?" This player struck out at a critical moment in the game. So what? It happens. Now ask, "Now what?" The answer was to serve someone else. So the next time you experience failure and resilience is now required on your part, stop and see what you can learn from the experience. Then take that experience and serve someone else. These are the type of resilient leaders who "get it" and become mighty.

Have you ever heard someone say when they walked through the door of their house and smelled what was cooking in the kitchen, they knew they were home? I have, and you likely have as well. Psychologists and brain experts claim the sense of smell is closely linked with memory. In fact, it is more so than any of the other senses. My favorite smell is pot roast after it has been in a crockpot for several hours. Oh my heavens, they should make a perfume called "Pot Roast!" I'm just saying.

For leaders who are feeling heat and pressure, or experiencing disappointment or constraints, you can learn a lot about what happens to meat when it is placed in a crockpot for an extended period of time.

Being placed in a crockpot forces the roast into a confined environment where heat will be applied. But rather than being a bad thing, the heat brings out the meat's natural juices. The juices then marinate the roast, causing the meat to tenderize and produce flavors and smells that draw you in. Afterward, you get to sit down to a great feast and enjoy the meal with others. Crockpotting is worth the wait.

This should comfort countless leaders reading this book. You may be in a job, department, or ministry you do not enjoy. You feel stuck and unable to utilize your strengths. Your opportunities for advancement are limited at best. It seems like you are just spinning your wheels while wasting your time in a dead-end job.

Or you may be feeling intense heat. Your boss is putting pressure on you, and no matter what you do, you cannot please him/her. The disrespect is palpable. Furthermore, despite your best efforts, positive results never seem to come your way. Each day, the pressure mounts more and more. You are constantly in fear if today is finally the day you will lose your job. But take comfort.

This heat and pressure are pulling things (juices) out of you that you do not even realize. You are becoming more tender (compassionate) and engaging as a leader. And there will eventually come a day when your resilience is rewarded, and a great number of people will sit down at a proverbial banquet of your leadership.

John Piper once said, "God is always doing 10,000 things in your life, and you may be aware of three of them." So if you are feeling heat or pressure and experiencing disappointment and constraints, get excited. You might just be in God's leadership crockpot.

COACH NICK SABAN

One leader who has definitely come out of a crockpot is Alabama's Nick Saban. On Halloween day, 2022, the legendary head coach turned seventy-one years old, but it appears he is only getting started. Entering his sixteenth season at Alabama, Coach Saban signed a $93.6 million contract extension through the 2030 season. In an ESPN article written by Chris Low, Coach Saban gave insight into what is required to stay resilient and have longevity as a leader.

First, to stay resilient and have longevity as a leader, you must first *feel* young. Proverbs 23:7 says, "For as he thinketh in his heart, so is he" (KJV). Coach Saban said, "First of all, I feel like a young man." It is said age is simply a number, but it is also a mindset. Coach Saban embodies that mindset.

You also must remain flexible. Leaders must reject rigidity and willingly change with the times. Coach Saban said, "You have to be flexible. I think that's one of the most important things about competitive sports. You know, the game has changed. The three-point shot changed basketball. So you either change with it or you fall behind." Coach Saban then applied this concept to college football. He noted, "The no-huddle changed football, RPOs changed football. If you don't sort of study the game and know the impact of these things and use them to your advantage, you're going to just completely get bypassed by a lot of folks."

Third, to stay resilient and have longevity as a leader, you must *choose* to be successful. Coach Saban said, "I heard it said that none of us are born winners, and none of us are born losers. We're all born choosers. So choosing the right things that are going to help you be successful ... that doesn't really change." You have the right to make whatever choices you wish. But you don't have the right to choose the consequences which come with those choices. You do not hear about consequences talked about much in political campaigns or many other venues anymore, but much of a someone's individual success is largely determined by their personal choices. Success does not happen by accident. It starts with a desire for success and then making the choices needed to achieve it. While everyone does not have the same starting point in their life or career, success is available for everyone if you consistently make the right choices. You make your choices, and then your choices make you.

As a leader it is also vitally important for you that one of your choices be to create value for others. Under the leadership of Nick Saban, 114 Alabama players have been selected in the NFL Draft through 2022, including forty-one first rounders. Alabama has also produced a first round pick in each of the last fourteen consecutive NFL Drafts, tying a NFL record. Coach Saban said, "The one thing, because of the brand that we have here, that players can see, is they can earn a tremendous amount of money because of the brand and because of the image that they can create using that brand to promote themselves, which has happened."

Resilience and longevity also require you to avoid personality conflicts and unnecessary distractions. Prior to the 2022 season, Coach Saban and Texas A&M head coach Jimbo Fisher engaged in a well-publicized squabble over recruiting and payments to players. Coach Saban said, "You know, things like that used to bother me a lot, and no one is happy about those things when they're said about you. But I've kind of learned that you really can't let this kind of stuff affect who you are." It appears both have moved on since that time. Coach Saban sure did as Alabama had the top-ranked recruiting class of 2023.

Coach Saban also has the mental toughness to focus on the right things. Coach Saban admitted, "I still can get hot under the collar every now and then, but I try to leave that to intangible things like giving effort, playing with toughness and finishing plays and not necessarily mental errors." He continued, "We don't have a lot of what I call energy vampires, guys that take all your time because they're not doing what they're supposed to do. We have a team that has bought in, and they're all trying to do the right thing."

Successful leadership requires developing a leadership culture in your organization. One of the signs of a healthy leadership culture is when your best players establish the team's level of intolerance for poor performance. Coach Saban concluded, "When the best players on your team are the best leaders, that's really a good thing."

To no one's surprise, Coach Saban said, "I wouldn't want to coach someplace that didn't have a high standard." Regardless of his age, experience, or amount of success he has had, Coach Saban will not be reduced to a level of mediocrity. He concluded, "I think I've become a better teacher. I think yelling and screaming at players in this day and age really goes in one ear and out the other. If you want them to really resonate on what you're saying, you just need to teach it, and sometimes, it works better if you do it individually than if you do it in front of other people. That's not something I considered in years past, several years past."

COACH GARETH SOUTHGATE

Another well-known coach also gives us a wonderful perspective on resilience. On June 26, 1996 Gareth Southgate experienced a career-defining failure. England was facing Germany in the UEFA Euro Semifinal soccer tournament. To put this in proper perspective, this sporting event is the equivalent of America's Super Bowl. Southgate, one of England's star players, lined up for a penalty kick to decide the game. If he makes the kick, the club has a chance to move onto the finals. If he misses, England is out of the tournament. Missing the kick would be a national embarrassment and let his entire team, family, friends, and nation down. It was as if Southgate's playing life had crystalized into this single, career-defining kick. Never had one swing of his leg meant so much. It was all on the line. No pressure, right?

Unfortunately, Southgate's worst fears were realized. Despite his best efforts, Southgate's kick was stopped by the German goalie. However, he would eventually move past his failure and go on to become the manager of England's World Cup team. But how did Southgate respond so well, and what can we learn from his resilience that can help us overcome missed expectations?

Prior to England's 2002 quarterfinal World Cup match against France, Southgate sat down with Fox Sports's Tom Rinaldi during the network's pre-match show. He said:

> We're all going to go through life and have huge setbacks. I feel fortunate that mine being in a professional sense up to this point. It built resilience because every stadium I played in, I was abused. Walking down the street, people (were) putting their windows down. So it builds mental resilience. I've been through some of the most difficult scenarios I can professionally and therefore, whatever happens I can handle and that does give you confidence in dealing with difficult situations.

The following are six lessons we learn from this great leader on the subject of failure:

First, failure is inevitable. It does not discriminate and sooner or later visits all of us. The question is not will we experience failure? The question is how will we handle it when it comes? A small failure is an inconvenience, but some failures will be huge. It is from the huge failures, the major setbacks, the ones which leave scars, that we learn from.

Second, failures can be gifts if you handle them right. Failures will make you bitter or better. Southgate felt fortunate to experience his failure. Third, failures are rarely final. They will either be setbacks or setups. If handled right, they can actually be learning opportunities for growth.

Fourth, failures build resilience. That is what this chapter is about. Southgate was heckled, abused, demeaned, and marginalized because of his missed kick. But pressure makes diamonds. Southgate used this experience to become wiser, kinder, and more empathetic to the players he now leads. Fifth, failure builds confidence. Because Southgate went through this experience, he now knows how to better handle difficult situations. If you let failure do its work in your life, you will be better equipped to handle the difficult situations when they come.

Southgate concluded, "Whatever happens in the World Cup, life is going to go on, and there are far more important things, but I've heard people use the phrase before, 'Ours' is the most important thing of the unimportant things in life.' I think that's a pretty good assessment for what it is." This leads to our final lesson from Southgate.

Sixth, failure needs to be contextualized. Once again, failure is usually not final. Many times, what you are going through is the most important of the unimportant things in your life. So learn from it, grow, get better, and move on to the next challenge.

STEPH CURRY AND P.J. O'BRIEN

Not all people in the world are like the great coaches mentioned above. There are many pre-resilient people in the world (is that a nice way to put it). They need someone to support them and be there when they are hurting. This is why at its best, leadership has the ability to elevate people. Leadership has the ability to inspire, make dreams come true, bring people together, and yes, even wipe away a few tears when necessary.

The Golden State Warriors superstar guard Steph Curry embodied the very best of leadership with a recent act of kindness. On March 8, 2022, the Denver Nuggets were hosting the Warriors. A ten-year-old fan named P.J. O'Brien showed up dressed in full-Warriors gear from head-to-toe and was there to cheer for Curry, her favorite player. She even had a poster made which read "Go Warriors MVP Steph Curry." Little did she know load management, players taking time off to rest their bodies and have sustainable energy for the long season, would cause her to become greatly disappointed. Curry would not be in attendance.

O'Brien was devastated and began to weep uncontrollably so much so it caught the attention of game officials and television personnel who were present and put her on camera. As suggested by the announcers, the Warriors decided to get P.J. and her family tickets for the next time the team visited the Mile High City. The great news for P.J. is she would not have wait long. The Warriors were returning just two nights later.

As mentioned previously, load management and players taking games off is not good for the league. This young fan clearly planned for months in advance to watch Curry. There was a time, financial (tickets, parking, merchandise, etc.) and emotional investment made by the family to attend a game, assuming he would play. The Warriors then sat him and several other star players out. Recognizing the level of disappointment this decision brought to P.J., the team and Curry himself went to work on a solution.

The solution was to not only purchase the family courtside seats, but to arrange a meeting between Curry and P.J. It was the perfect solution for mending a young fan's broken heart.

As game time approached, P.J. returned to a front row seat, wearing the same outfit and with the same sign. It was then that she received a surprise visit from none other than Curry himself. O'Brien then openly wept again. But this time, not with tears of disappointment, but tears of joy as Curry spent several minutes with her.

After the game, Curry said, "This is what the NBA is all about." As a representative and one of the primary faces of his industry, Curry knew how much joy it would bring P.J. and how much goodwill it would bring to the league. He had every right to have stayed in the locker room and focused on his pre-game routine. No one would have thought less of him. At that moment, however, P.J. *was* his job and his primary responsibility. This was just another example of why the NBA could not have a better ambassador than Curry. He teaches us that the best solutions are personal, specific to the issue, cost something, and most importantly, fix the problem. P.J. had an experience she will never forget.

Successful leaders are always on the lookout for opportunities to build the resilience of Shammah in themselves and others. By doing such things you have a chance to become mighty and move yourself and others from pandemic to progress.

CHAPTER 3 STUDY AND DISCUSSION QUESTIONS

Are you as a leader willing to stand alone when necessary? If so, give us a time you have needed to do so in the past.

_____

_____

_____

Are you in a storm, coming out of a storm, or going into one? Whatever the case may be, is it a storm of perfection or a storm of correction?

_____

_____

_____

How often do you complain about the cost leadership requires? What causes you to do so in those times?

_____

_____

_____

How do you help those who are not as resilient as you are?

_____

_____

_____

Do you embrace "hard" things? Do you run toward hard or from it and why?

_____

_____

_____

CHAPTER 4
Teamwork

And three of the thirty chief men went down and came about harvest time to David at the cave of Adullam, when a band of Philistines was encamped in the Valley of Rephaim. David was then in the stronghold, and the garrison of the Philistines was then at Bethlehem. And David said longingly, "Oh, that someone would give me water to drink from the well of Bethlehem that is by the gate!" Then the three mighty men broke through the camp of the Philistines and drew water out of the well of Bethlehem that was by the gate and carried and brought it to David. But he would not drink of it. He poured it out to the Lord and said, "Far be it from me, O Lord, that I should do this. Shall I drink the blood of the men who went at the risk of their lives?" Therefore he would not drink it. These things the three mighty men did.

—2 Samuel 23:13–17 (ESV)

In the summer of 1992, a collection of professional basketball players (and one collegiate player) from the United States were assembled. Their talents were so prodigious that people were in awe and flocked in overflow crowds just to get a glimpse of them whether walking down the street or playing on the basketball court. Their every move was followed and analyzed. This collection of basketball talent destroyed every opponent they faced and easily won the Olympic gold medal. All eleven professional players were eventually inducted into the Hall of Fame. Led by legendary players like Michael Jorden, Magic Johnson, and Charles Barkley, this group of athletes became known as The Dream Team.

Even though he was in the wilderness, David assembled his own "Dream Team" as well. They would become known as his Mighty Men. In addition to the three men we've already met (Josheb-basshebeth, Eleazar, and Shammah), the Bible goes on to mention Abishai and Benaiah (who we will discuss in later chapters), as well as thirty-two other prominent warriors listed below in verses 24–39:

> *Asahel the brother of Joab was one of the thirty; Elhanan the son of Dodo of Bethlehem, Shammah of Harod, Elika of Harod, Helez the Paltite, Ira the son of Ikkesh of Tekoa, Abiezer of Anathoth, Mebunnai the Hushathite, Zalmon the Ahohite, Maharai of Netophah, Heleb the son of Baanah of Netophah, Ittai the son of Ribai of Gibeah of the people of Benjamin, Benaiah of Pirathon, Hiddai of the brooks of Gaash, Abi-albon the Arbathite, Azmaveth of Bahurim, Eliahba the Shaalbonite, the sons of Jashen, Jonathan, Shammah the Hararite, Ahiam the son of Sharar the Hararite, Eliphelet the son of Ahasbai of Maacah, Eliam the son of Ahithophel the Gilonite, Hezro of Carmel, Paarai the Arbite, Igal the son of Nathan of Zobah, Bani the Gadite, Zelek the Ammonite, Naharai of Beeroth, the armor-bearer of Joab the son of Zeruiah, Ira the Ithrite, Gareb the Ithrite, Uriah the Hittite: thirty-seven in all."* (ESV)

What we learn from the Mighty Men is that you if you want to become mighty and move from the pandemic to progress, it requires teamwork. David could not get out of the wilderness alone. Neither can you.

But just as The Dream Team had Jordan, Magic, and Barkley, David had Josheb-basshebeth, Eleazar, and Shammah. This was a select group. In fact, when describing Abishai in verse 19, it says, "He was the most renowned of the thirty and became their commander, but he did not attain to the three." Regarding Benaiah in verses 22–23, the Bible records the following, "These things did Benaiah the son of Jehoiada, and won a name beside the three mighty men. He was renowned among the thirty, but he did not attain to the three."

As great as the other thirty-four Mighty Men were, there was something special about the three, Josheb-basshebeth, Eleazar, and Shammah. So what was it? We get a picture of what that was in verses 13–17 when these three, who did heroic and awe-inspiring things individually, came together collectively.

These three men deeply loved David and were loyal to him. As I read verses 13–17, I imagine the four sitting together one day when David leans back, hot and thirsty from life in the wilderness, and reflected (paraphrase), "Man, would I like to have that cold water from the well at Bethlehem." It was a passing comment. He probably didn't think anything else about it, and they carried on with the remainder of their conversation.

Because of Josheb-basshebeth, Eleazar, and Shammah's love for David, his passing comment took residence in their mind. Though David forgot his statement, they did not. It appears they came together afterward and hatched an audacious plan. They proceeded to fight through the Philistine army; in fact, it says they "broke through the camp" and made their way behind enemy lines to the well of Bethlehem. They drew the cold, refreshing water and then fought back through the Philistine camp a second time to return to their beloved leader David.

I can only imagine the look on David's face when he looked at his battle-wearied friends and inquired to where they have been. I see the chief of the three, Josheb-basshebeth, saying, "David, do remember when you longed to drink the refreshing waters from the well of Bethlehem.? Well here you go!"

David probably asked the three, "Are you crazy? Why did you do this?" To which I imagined they would answer, "Because we love you. We'd do anything for you, including risking our lives."

David was obviously overwhelmed with love and gratitude. Remember, when David was in Saul's palace, he was despised for being a successful warrior and even had spears thrown at him while attempting to soothe the king. He was despised, and his life was at risk for simply carrying out his assignments with excellence. Now in the wilderness, his finest men were risking their lives in service to him. What a change. David's only response was worship.

In the modern Western world, we do not understand drink offerings. Today's readers would think, "What a waste. We did all that work for nothing." But the drink offering represented many things in biblical times, including an absolute sacrifice of worship to God. Josheb-basshebeth, Eleazar, and Shammah would view this as one of the greatest compliments they could ever receive. Their actions resulted in spontaneous worship from the leader whom they served with excellence and loved deeply.

GEORGIA BULLDOGS

Everyone reading this book wants to be part of an elite team. No one wants to give their lives to average pursuits. A leader wants to make a difference with their one and only life, and we know to do this, we need an elite team around us. Our vision is too great to be accomplished alone. So what are the qualities of a group of individuals known as an elite team?

On the December 3, 2022 broadcast of ESPN's *College Gameday*, defending national champion Georgia Bulldogs head coach Kirby Smart was interviewed prior to his team's SEC Championship game against the LSU Tigers. Coach Smart knows something about elite teams and gave us a unique glimpse into what is needed to achieve championship-level results.

Coach Smart said, "We've got some kids who are really good leaders. They buy in to the organization (and) the culture. They've done it. We give them the tools. We give them the X's and O's but they push each other and hold each other accountable."

He then added:

> A lot of time in the off-season. We do a lot of structuring. We make guys talk. We make guys understand what the guy before them sacrificed. Make it about the team. That's what elite teams do. They worry about the next game, not the last game. They worry about the team, not the individual. We sell that really hard in the off-season. I don't know if it's a perfect remedy (as) our kids have issues, too, but our kids have been resilient.

As we break down Coach Smart's comments, we learn ten things elite teams do. First is the principle followed by his quote.

1. Elite teams are made up of many good leaders. "We've got some kids who are really good leaders."

2. Elite teams are aligned and attuned. "They buy in to the organization (and) the culture."

3. Elite teams have elite coaching. "We give them the tools. We give them the X's and O's."

4. Elite teams are accountable to each other. "They push each other and hold each other accountable."

5. Elite teams have elite preparation. They are elite in private when no one is watching. "A lot of time in the off-season . . . We sell that really hard in the off-season."

6. Elite teams have elite communication. "We do a lot of structuring. We make guys talk."

7. Elite teams are not entitled. "We make guys understand what the guy before them sacrificed."

8. Elite teams elevate the team above the individual. "Make it about the team . . . They worry about the team, not the individual."

9. Elite teams have short memories and are focused on the future. "They worry about the next game, not the last game."

10. Elite teams are resilient. "I don't know if it's a perfect remedy (as) our kids have issues, too, but our kids have been resilient."

What is one lesson you learned from Coach Smart that if implemented *today* will make you a better team?

SAN FRANCISCO 49ERS

In an October 6, 2022, article written by Ted Nguyen for *The Athletic*, he takes a look at that year's San Francisco 49ers' defense and why it has a chance to be historic. Whether you lead a church, business, nonprofit, educational or athletic organization, the lessons learned can help you build a more effective and high-performing team.

First, great teams have great players. This is not complicated. You cannot have success without them. John Wooden said, "I'd rather have a lot of talent and a little experience than a lot of experience and a little talent."

Coach Lou Holtz added, "I've coached teams with good players and I've coached teams with bad players. I'm a better coach when I have good players!" Nguyen noted the 49ers had blue-chip players at every level of defense—the defensive line, linebackers, and secondary. Simply put, they are loaded with talent.

Second, great teams have players who play to their strengths. If you want a bad team, simply have a large number of people doing what they are *not* good at. That is a recipe for failure. Nguyen writes, "Defensive coordinator DeMeco Ryans understands the strengths and weaknesses of his players and puts them in a position to succeed." Do you know the strengths of those on your team and have you put them in positions to be successful? If not, stop reading this page right now and develop a plan to do so.

Third, great teams continually make adjustments. Yesterday's solutions do not solve today's problems. The world is too fluid for rigid leaders to be successful. Today's most successful teams, those who are making progress, are nimble and "can make necessary schematic adjustments."

Fourth, great teams know who fits best into their culture and hires only those people. Culture is who you hire. The problem with many organizations is they don't know who they are, and their hiring practices reflect as much. The 49ers know who they want from a size, skill, and mentality perspective. Nguyen wrote, "The 49ers seek out big, explosive athletes who can change directions." Do you have an ideal employee profile for the type of individuals you want to add to your organization? If not, get together with your team and make one up today!

Fifth, great teams are a team of leaders. No matter what type of organization you may be, you can never have enough quality leaders. The 49ers' head coach, Kyle Shanahan, is generally recognized as one of the brightest head coaches in the league, and Ryans will be on everyone's short list for head coaching opportunities in 2023.

And then there is defensive line coach Kris Kocurek. What is interesting about the previous point of the 49ers wanting "big, explosive athletes who can change directions" is what is not said. Skill was not listed. Obviously, they want a high level of skill, but if the players have a certain mental and athletic makeup, Coach Kocurek is tasked with teaching them the schematic elements of their craft.

Another great leader for the 49ers is their offensive line coach and run game coordinator Chris Foerster. Most people think creativity in professional football is found in the passing game. But if you watch any 49ers game, their use of formations, personnel groupings, and how they get the ball into the hands of their playmakers through the running game is every bit as creative.

In a September 30, 2022, press conference, Foerster addressed the importance of little things when it comes to individual and team success. He said:

> I look at fundamentals . . . I can see things that while it may be productive, it may not be good in four weeks when he starts developing a library of plays. Dude, if you don't fix this stuff now, there is going to be a problem. There are those things. Everybody has them. You're constantly picking at the guy. Trent (future Hall of Fame tackle Williams), if you don't fix this . . . When you get against that elite guy on the road with a silent count, that's going to be a problem.

Foerster continues, "They all have their little things. I could probably punch list three things for every guy. Work on these three things in practice every single day and you'll be a lot happier with our production going forward."

Regardless of your profession or area of discipline, to become mighty and move from pandemic to progress, you need to get a coach like

Chris Foerster in your life. Great coaches look at your fundamentals and notice bad habits, which are developing. They notice our good and bad tendencies and relentlessly address them by creating individualized plans for improvement, punch lists if you will. Bottom line, everybody gets better with a coach.

Finally, great teams have depth. Nguyen writes, "what makes the 49ers special is how deep their rotation is." Depth gives your team margin in case of injuries, resignations, or individual poor performance. It also gives you a developmental pipeline, ensuring long-term success. You want your team to be green (continually having young talent) and growing (proven talent). Depth gives you this possibility.

ANDREW WIGGINS

Smart leaders place a high priority on creating a winning culture when team building. To do this you need a depth of people who are known as great teammates. One such teammate is the aforementioned Golden State Warriors forward Andrew Wiggins. In fact, throughout the 2022 NBA Finals against the Boston Celtics, he was the team's second-best player behind Steph Curry. Game 5, in particular, became another defining moment for him.

In the team's 104–94 victory, Wiggins had twenty-six points, thirteen rebounds, two steals, two assists, and one block. Warriors guard Klay Thompson said, "I mean, buying in is one of the biggest keys to success in this league, and for what Andrew did tonight, I mean, we don't get—we don't get more excited than when Wiggs dunks on somebody. And that really uplifts the whole team and the Bay Area." We learn five things about being a great teammate from Thompson's comments:

First, great teammates buy in to the organization's mission and vision. They put the interests of the organization ahead of their own personal interests. Great teammates become catalysts for making the organization's mission and vision a reality. They do this by knowing what their strengths are and have learned how to best leverage those for the success of others.

Second, great teammates attract people who are also great teammates. Birds of a feather flock together. Like begets like. Having a team of great teammates is one of the biggest keys to success in any industry. You simply can't win with a team full of knuckleheads. You can't do it. Selfish, irresponsible, and lazy teammates accelerate your organization's failure.

Third, great teammates celebrate the success of their fellow teammates. I loved how Thompson said how much everyone gets excited when Wiggins excels. Most people do a great job weeping with those who weep but often a poor job rejoicing with those who rejoice. Don't be too quick to pass judgment on these self-focused individuals. How well do you respond when a teammate in your department has greater success than you? Are you happy for them, or do you become jealous or envious?

Fourth, great teammates uplift their entire team. They put wind in the sails of others. Great teammates ease burdens and lift the loads of their coworkers. They are the rising tide which lifts all ships. A fifth thing about great teammates is consistency, you can count on them every day. Curry said, "He's embraced the challenge of consistency and what he's capable of doing on both ends of the floor."

Fifth, great teammates are defined by their ability to bring out the best in others. Let's read a few of thoughts from Wiggins himself. He said, "I feel like being here; it's a winning culture. They have won before, and they have dominated the NBA. When I got here, they put you in position to succeed. They always bring out the best in you." Wiggins concluded, "They want the best for you. You know, supportive."

Many people have the potential to be great teammates but, unfortunately, are in less-than-ideal situations. These individuals are often diamonds in the rough. Smart leaders are able to identify these distressed assets and secure their services. Warriors Coach Steve Kerr said. "But I think it's a reminder that for every—almost every player—in the NBA, circumstances are everything. You kind of need to find the right place, the right teammates, that kind of stuff. Wiggs has been a great fit."

Circumstances are often everything. I can speak from personal experience as I have succeeded in some environments and failed in others. The difference in most cases was my skills fit the task or assignment required. Most importantly, they believed in me and were personally invested in my success. I hope you find a similar culture to demonstrate your skills. Now let's look at what happens when you hire someone who is the opposite of a someone like Andrew Wiggins.

INVASIVE SPECIES

Environmental science project manager Ian Bartoszek and biologist Ian Easterling were walking through the Florida Everglades in December 2021 when they heard a rustling in the bushes. What they found was a shocking discovery. The two found an eighteen-foot Burmese python weighing a remarkable 215 pounds. This was the largest invasive species ever caught in America, shattering the previous record of 140 pounds. It took their team twenty minutes to apprehend the snake.

What also surprised the scientists was what was found inside the python. The snake's contents included the remains of a white tail deer along with 122 python eggs.

After being introduced into the Florida ecosystem in the 1970s as a result of the exotic pet trade, the US Geological Survey (USGS) now estimates tens of thousands of pythons live in Florida. The Burmese python is now considered Florida's apex predator, even more so than alligators.

Florida governor Ron DeSantis said in a June 17, 2022, press conference, "It's just unbelievable what they will ravage when they're there. These snakes are destroying the natural food chain, and you can't have a healthy environment without a healthy food chain." The USGS called the Burmese python "one of the most concerning invasive species in the Everglades National Park." Florida has set aside over $3 million for the removal of the species.

So what does this have to do with leadership and teamwork? Well, it has everything to do with establishing a healthy culture in your organization. As previously mentioned, culture is who you hire. Let me say that again, culture is who you hire. You may currently have a healthy workplace culture. If so, it should come with a warning label. Your culture should be protected and intensely guarded. By inserting an "invasive species" (hiring the wrong person) into your ecosystem, your entire culture could be disrupted or destroyed.

The wrong hire could destroy trust, lower performance, create divisions in the organization, cause good employees to leave, change your messaging, create negative or sideways energy, lose customers, and harm your brand.

There is much to learn from the state of Florida. If an "invasive species" enters your workplace ecosystem, immediately deal with the issue. Otherwise, your problems will grow to overwhelming proportions, and your entire culture will be severely impacted.

TOXIC BOSSES

The worst type of an "invasive species" is a toxic leader. On August 23, 1973, four individuals were taken captive when Jan-Erik Olsson attempted a bank robbery in Stockholm, Sweden. Over the course of a six-day standoff with the police, several of the captives became sympathetic to Olsson. This condition of developing compassion, sympathy, and even positive feelings for one's captors became known as Stockholm Syndrome.

The Stockholm Syndrome is a coping mechanism which helps people deal with abusive (and sometimes life-threatening) individuals. These situations could be as extreme as the hostage situation from 1973 but could also include abusive or toxic relationships in the home, workplace, or athletic arena.

I have worked for toxic bosses before. There is a good chance many people reading this have, as well. Candidly, there were times I felt I was experiencing Stockholm Syndrome as I continually made excuses for the behavior of these harmful individuals. Fortunately, toxic leaders can't help but eventually lose all their influence and ultimately lose their leadership positions as well. To help identify toxic leaders, the following is a composite picture of bosses I have seen who harm those they are called to serve:

Toxic bosses have explosive tempers. There is a constant state of volatility surrounding these leaders. They are angry and easily set off. As a result, their team members walk on eggshells around them. You never know what will trigger their hostility.

Toxic bosses lead by fear. They hold people's jobs over their heads. Unreasonable expectations and constant threats become institutionalized. As a result, their employees lack any sense of security and constantly fear for their jobs.

Toxic bosses breed unhealthy competition among teammates. People are constantly compared to and pitted against each other. As a result, the workplace lacks trust and unity. Gossip is a constant in toxic environments.

Toxic bosses tear people down. They are bullies and manipulative. Rather than developing people and building them up, they often target certain employees they view as weak and continually verbally abuse them both to their face and behind their back to others. They backstab. Toxic bosses, at their core, are cowards.

Toxic bosses never take responsibility for their failures. "That was my fault." "I made a mistake." "Please forgive me." "I need to get better." These phrases are not part of the vernacular of toxic bosses. And if they come even close to an apology, they will then use the word *but* and blame others for their behavior.

Toxic bosses are reckless. Toxicity has an absence of boundaries. They are reckless with their language and how they treat the opposite sex. My experience is they have also been reckless in every area of their life, including their language, diet, alcohol consumption, finances, and questionable viewing habits.

Toxic bosses rarely acknowledge excellent work. Their toxicity has eclipsed their ability to recognize the contributions of others. Toxic bosses have unhappy personal lives. You can't compartmentalize toxicity. A toxic boss often has a toxic marriage and toxic relationships with their children. The worst part, toxic bosses are more comfortable in unhealthy conflict than in peace. Therefore, they often create strife even if none exists.

Toxic bosses also withhold blessings from their employees. Toxicity and generosity simply cannot occupy the same space. Finally, toxic bosses have high turnover. Toxicity is fundamentally unsustainable.

Emotionally healthy individuals will self-select out of toxic environments. Toxic bosses will also lose many clients and strategic partnerships.

If you work for a toxic boss, you do not have to succumb to Stockholm Syndrome. You are a someone who can escape. In a post-pandemic world there are too many other options out there for you. The following is the type of a leader you should want to work for.

THE ROLE, DUTY, AND EXPECTATION OF A COACH

Billy Graham once said, "A coach will impact more people in one year than the average person will in an entire lifetime." If this statement is true, and I believe it is, then it is important to understand what the role, duty, and expectation of a coach is.

As mentioned previously, I participate in a weekly Zoom Bible study with approximately seventy high school, college, and professional baseball scouts and coaches. During one of our times together, White Sox scout Kevin Burrell taught a lesson on the subject of baptism. Kevin pointed out that baptism is an outward sign you are playing for a new team (Christianity) and have a new coach (Jesus Christ).

To connect the dots for this very specific audience, he asked, "What is the role, duty, and expectation of a coach?" The following are the answers from some of the top scouts and coaches in baseball:

A coach is a model. Lee Seras, scouting supervisor for the Cincinnati Reds said, "Become a model and a leader." A coach trains and develops players. Luke Wrenn, retired scout from the Seattle Mariners, Boston Red Sox, and Arizona Diamondbacks, said a coach's job is "to develop the players to be the best that they can be." A coach imparts knowledge. Wrenn added that a coach is "to be an example to them and to impart knowledge."

A coach meets you where you are at. Kevin Wilson, one of the most sought-after hitting consultants in the game and currently working with minor and major league players from twenty different MLB organizations, said, "Meet them where they're at." A coach creates a path for you and guides you in it. Kevin added that a coach will "guide them in a path you want them to go in."

A coach is a mentor. Rich Sparks, scout for the Oakland A's, said, "Be a mentor." A coach teaches you to take responsibility. Rick Robinson, former college baseball coach for over twenty years and currently a missionary with SCORE International said, "Teach them to take responsibility." A coach teaches you to operate within the context of a team. Rick concluded by saying a coach also teaches you "how to participate and operate as a team player."

Burrell then summarized by tying these traits back to the Holy Spirit's work in a person's life after salvation. He said:

> The message of baptism is I have a new coach and this new coach is going to help me. He's going to model for me. He's going to help train me. He's going to help me reach my abilities as a new follower of Christ. He's going to mentor me. All the above. He's going to care for me. He's going to discipline me . . . That new coach is the Holy Spirit that abides within you and he's going to walk with you and he's going to talk with you, and he's going to train you, and he's going to teach you, and he's going to lead you every day.

That is the type of leader we should all want to follow.

Let's now shift from something solid as a rock like a personal relationship with Jesus Christ to literal shifting sand.

SANDCASTLES

Every team gets better when a leader gets better. I was reminded of this truth by reading a recent article from TheConversation.com about of all things, constructing the perfect sandcastle. The parallels between constructing the perfect sandcastle and becoming the perfect coach or team leader are startling. Allow me to explain.

When constructing the perfect sandcastle, author Joseph Scalia writes that water is the key. He notes:

> Water is cohesive, meaning that water likes to stick to water. But water also sticks to or climbs up certain surfaces. Look at a half-full glass of water and you will see the water going up the insides of the glass a little. Gravity still holds the water in the glass, but the water is trying to climb up and wet the surface. This tiny power struggle is what makes sandcastles possible. Right where the air and water meet, there's surface tension.

We learn several leadership lessons from the paragraph above about what leaders do to make teams more successful:

As mentioned with Andrew Wiggins, leaders attract other leaders. Scalia teaches us water likes to stick to water. Similarly, leaders like to stick with other leaders. As your organization begins to build a leadership culture, it will attract more and more leaders.

Leaders are always breaking new ground. Few people knew that water is always looking to break out of the glass it is contained in. It is only gravity that holds it down. Leaders are the same way. They are always looking to "break out of the glass." Leaders are always breaking boundaries and taking new ground. Just as there is always tension between water and gravity, there is a constant battle between leaders and the status quo.

Scalia continues by writing, "The quantity of water in the sand controls the size and strength of the water bridges. Too little water equals little bridges between the sand grains. More water, and the size and number of bridges grows, increasing the suction holding the sand grains together. The result is perfect sandcastle sand." This leads to perhaps the three most important parallels.

The most successful teams and organizations have the most quality leaders. As we have discussed with the San Francisco 49ers, you can never have too many leaders. Just as the quantity of water in the sand controls the size and strength of the sand, the quantity of leaders your organization has determines its size and strength. The goal of every organization should be to acquire and raise up as many leaders as possible. The more leaders you have, the more successful your team will be.

Growing leaders build growing organizations. You need more than just quantity. The capacity of your leaders will determine the capacity of your organization. Therefore, one of your goals as an organization should be leadership development and the personal growth of your leaders. Just as more water increases the size of the castle, the size of the capacity of your leaders allows your "castle" to grow as well.

Finally, what makes the perfect sandcastle is the more water you have, the more suction that is created, and thus the sand holds together. That is what great leaders do. Great leaders are like duct tape. They hold everything together. Great leaders solve problems and create beauty out of ashes. They bring a sense of calm and security to everyone in your organization.

KYLIAN MBAPPE

Twenty-five years ago, I attended church with an individual who was the chief marketing officer of one of America's leading companies. He was deeply respected and admired by those in our church, so much so no one ever asked him to volunteer in their area of ministry. It was not unlike the pretty girl who never got asked out for a date in high school because everyone thought she would decline.

I asked our business administrator why this high-capacity leader did not hold a position at our church. The response was quite insightful and a learning experience for me. I was told, "Someone on that level does not want a title; they want influence."

On May 23, 2022 soccer superstar Kylian Mbappe signed the richest contract in the sport's history to stay with Paris Saint-Germain (PSG). The following were the key points for how and why Mbappe made his decision. Elite leaders have many options, so these items teach us several things about recruiting individuals who could potentially transform your team.

First, financial considerations matter a great deal, but it is not the only determining factor when selecting which organization to join. Mbappe was presented extraordinarily generous compensation packages from both PSG and Real Madrid. Though he ultimately accepted a three-year contract from PSG worth €57 million net per season, along with various bonuses potentially worth €100 million over the three years of the deal, there were other items which impacted his decision.

One had to do with Mbappe's inner circle. Mbappe's parents and lawyer were key advisors. He was also being advised by some of the most powerful people in France, including the country's president Emmanuel Macron. When recruiting elite talent to your team, you must also recruit those closest to the leader. For instance, if you were recruiting me to join your organization, you would also need to recruit my wife. You must influence those who influence the leader.

Also, John Maxwell's Law of Connection teaches that you should always touch a person's heart before asking for their hand. Mbappe said, "Leaving my country wasn't the right thing. There's a sentimental aspect to this, and the sporting project has changed as well." Never discount the heart attachment involved in the decision-making process of elite leaders. You must learn what the leader laughs about, cries about, and dreams about.

Finally and most importantly, elite leaders want greater influence and larger platforms. As told in the earlier story, elite leaders are not interested in personal titles. They've already had those things, probably multiple times over. They want to influence leaders and make a generational impact. Mbappe was given the "keys" to the club. He will now be involved in management and personnel decisions. At twenty-three years old, Mbappe has become the face of PSG.

If you are looking to add an elite leader to your team, one who could truly transform your organization, are you willing to give them the keys to the organization and make them the face of your company? If not, rest assured another organization likely will.

But don't forget the sustainability of your leadership is primarily built, not just on adding elite talent, but also on your continual ability to add value to people already on your team. If you are not adding value to their lives, not improving their current circumstances, not helping them get to a brighter tomorrow, and not helping make their dreams come true, why should they continue to follow you? If you cannot do those things, they will also follow someone else who will.

WORLD CUP 2022

On Sunday, December 18, 2022, Argentina won the 2022 World Cup by defeating France in the shootout, following a 3–3 score. Some are considering it the greatest match in World Cup history. What made the contest so compelling was the team's two mega-stars, Lionel Messi and Mbappe, performed at an elite level.

Throughout the tournament, Messi would score seven goals and assist on three others. But it was when the stakes were highest that he performed his best. In the semi-finals against Croatia, he scored one goal and had a mesmerizing assist which will go down as one of the iconic plays in soccer history. Then in the championship game, Messi scored two goals and had the opening goal in the shootout.

Though France finished as the Cup's runner-up, Mbappe won the Golden Boot as the tournament's leading goal scorer with eight. Similar to Messi, he played his best when it mattered most. Mbappe became the second player in World Cup history to have a hat trick in the Final.

The lesson leaders can take is what separates superstars like Messi and Mbappe, as well as the superstars in any industry, is the ability to execute under pressure. Big-time players make big-time plays in big-time games. To perform at an elite level in high-pressure situations, you must focus on execution, proper thinking, and accomplishment. But part of elite performance is adding value to your teammates.

One of my go-to resources for leadership growth is the @CoachTheCoaches Twitter feed. Their content is a "resource for coaches to help them add value to their student-athletes, while maximizing the strengths and minimizing the weaknesses of their teams." On August 29, 2018, they tweeted, "Commit to adding value to everyone and everything you come in contact with. Focus on making everyone around you better by putting their interests, their needs and their goals first." As I read their words and broke down its content, I gleaned the following lessons on how leaders can best add value to those on their teams:

"Commit"—Adding value to others is a choice. Leaders must make an intentional decision, a commitment, to add value to all those they come in contact with.

"Adding value"—Leadership is not neutral. You are either adding value or extracting value from your teammates and everyone in your area of influence.

"To everyone"—Adding value is nondiscriminatory. Successful leaders cannot pick and choose who they add value to. Each person you meet is a stewardship of opportunity.

"And everything"—In addition to adding value to your teammates and everyone you meet, you also have the leadership responsibility to add value to every organization you deal with. Every room a leader walks in should become better because they are there.

"You come in contact with"—Many people think *love* is the most important word in the English language. It is actually *relationships* because relationships are the tracks love runs on. Adding value is a relational decision.

"Focus"—Adding value to people does not happen by default. People do not default into adding value. They default into extracting value. Once again, it is intentional decision.

"On making everyone around you better"—How do you know if you added value or not? Did the person or organization you interacted with get better? A leader's success is found in the success of others.

"By putting their interests"—Adding value is an act of generosity. It is a demonstration of kindness and consideration of others.

"Their needs"—Leaders can best add value to their teams by putting their interests above their own. The best way to know what your team's needs are is simply by asking them.

"And their goals"—Leaders must also know what their people aspire to. Zig Ziglar famously said, "If you help people get what they want, they will help you get what you want."

"First"—The first responsibility of leadership is adding value to others. It is why leaders exist. What is one thing you can do today to better add value to those on your team?

"The best teams have this"—The above listing provides a wonderful checklist to not only self-evaluate but to also help you become the best leader and team moving forward.

I have mentioned the baseball scouts and coaches Bible study I participate in several times. In one of the lessons, NorthStar Church Senior Pastor Mike Linch made a powerful point saying, "Great coaches never miss a teachable moment." This is why when one of the people on the call, Coach Keith Madison, spoke on the subject of teambuilding, I took notes.

If you are not familiar with Coach Madison, let me introduce you to him. While serving as head baseball coach at the University of Kentucky for twenty-five years, he amassed 737 wins and has been inducted into three Halls of Fame: Kentucky High School Baseball Hall of Fame, University of Kentucky Hall of Fame, and the American Baseball Coaches Association Hall of Fame. In 2013, Coach Madison was honored with the Lefty Gomez Award. He then retired from coaching in 2003 and joined the team at SCORE International.

By working with SCORE International, Coach Madison combines two of the passions in his life: his faith and baseball. He reaches hundreds of college and high school baseball coaches and friends through his biweekly devotions and has spoken to thousands of coaches and players in sixteen states and the Dominican Republic.

One of the anchor verses of Mike's study that day was Matthew 20:28 which states, "even as the Son of Man came not to be served but to serve, and to give his life as a ransom for many." Commenting on this verse, Coach Madison said, "Putting yourself (as the leader) on a pedestal, you lose connection with your players. When you get in the trenches and ask great questions, you connect with your players. The best teams have this."

There is that phrase again, "the best teams have this." The following are four primary takeaways from Coach Madison's statement along the verse mentioned:

1. I can't say it enough. The only sustainable leadership model is a servant-leadership one.

2. Leaders have a choice whether to be servant leaders or not. They can choose a self-serving pedestal or to get into the trenches and serve their teams.

3. Great leaders ask great questions. They are curious, especially about what is happening with their people.

4. The one thing all high-performing teams have is they are led by servant-leaders who are in the trenches with their teams. You can only connect with people when you are with them, not from the corner office or green room.

Are you such a leader and teambuilder? Many leaders are not. In fact, some leaders are not teambuilders; they are actually team destroyers. I was recently speaking with a friend whose organization lost several of its top producers. What was alarming to me was not just the fact he lost so many talented individuals at once and the significant impact it would have on his organization, what was most disconcerting was he did not seem to care. It was as if it was simply just another day at the office. Sadly, this is not an isolated incident. I have seen this scenario played out countless times before in numerous organizations.

A loss of talented and productive people does not have to happen. If my friend would have just understood this thirteen-step process I am about to outline for you, his organization would still have these individuals in the fold and their future would not be in doubt.

THIRTEEN-STEP PROCESS FOR LOSING TALENTED PEOPLE AND TOP PRODUCERS

1. Organizations do not even recognize in the first place they have talented people and top producers. They simply cannot spot talent. Once again, you also can't lead from the corner office or green room. If my friend would have just been among his customers, he would have known the impact those who left were making. But because my friend led from a position of isolation, he listened to the wrong voices and misevaluated the talent he had. Consequently, he made faulty assumptions and many of the following mistakes listed.

2. Organizations prioritize previous relationships over progress. You can't run your organization like high school. Cliques cannot dominate your culture. It is easy to confuse longevity with stagnation. The "cool kids" need to include others, even if they are new, better, more talented, or have a different personality type than they do. And because they either don't like them personally or feel threatened by them professionally, they listen to the wrong voices and commit the following error.

3. Organizations exclude talented people and top producers from key decisions. As previously mentioned, top producers don't want titles, they want respect and influence. Do not freeze them out. It is disrespectful to exclude them from important meetings and not invite them into the decision-making process. When you leapfrog talented people and top producers, you will lose them to organizations who value their opinions.

4. Organizations prioritize their persona over progress. Talented people and top producers are always advancing the organization. This is bothersome to the existing establishment because they like things the way they are. In fact, they put into place many of the policies and procedures that are being challenged. They confuse questions with questioning, which leads to the next point.

5. Organizations prioritize peace over progress. Movement requires friction. Issues must be addressed. The status quo is not acceptable to talented people and top producers. But many times, they face an organizational establishment which is unwilling to change. As previously mentioned, this establishment freezes out talented people and does not want them in future discussions. As a result, the talent eventually leaves for other opportunities.

6. Organizations minimize the contributions of talented people and top producers. Because the establishment is feeling threatened and challenged, they minimize their contributions. They are told what they are producing is unsatisfactory even though it is at a high level. Furthermore, they are told they lack skill, work ethic, or an understanding of what is needed. But they don't stop there.

7. Organizations minimize the concerns of talented people and top producers. Not only does the establishment minimize their contributions, they also minimize their concerns. Their ideas are dismissed and issues they bring up are tabled. The establishment "puts

a pin in it." Talented people and top producers eventually roll their eyes and say, "They just don't get it. In fact, they'll never get it."

8. The organization is led by absentee or distracted leaders. Everything rises and falls on leadership. Other items have eclipsed the importance of the organization. This is major problem because the top producers are giving their life to the organization's mission and vision. But the leaders are not. The culture is officially unhealthy and unsustainable.

9. The organization and its leaders have stopped growing. So goes the leaders, so goes the organization. Once again, the status quo is good enough. What was average is now considered excellent, but not to the talented people and top producers. Average is not excellent; and it is, in fact, unacceptable. Frustration mounts because growing people will not follow nongrowing leaders. This is because nongrowing leaders cannot lead growing organizations. Therefore, their talented people and top producers leave for organizations with growing leaders.

10. Organizations lose talented people and top producers when they do not lead them. Talented people and top producers understand the value of leadership. They crave it. Even more so, they demand it. They are angry when they don't get it. Peyton Manning said in the NFL Films documentary *Summer School,* "I like to be coached and I get frustrated when I'm not coached or corrected on a mistake I've made." Much like Manning, if they cannot find coaching at their existing organization, they will seek it out elsewhere if necessary.

11. Organizations don't have a pathway for advancement. Talented people and top producers are always taking new ground, both in the marketplace and in the office. If they are stonewalled or frozen out with no new ground to take, they will find alternative plots of land elsewhere.

12. Organizations do not properly pay talented people and top producers. Talent is in high demand in our society because it is at such a premium. If you are not willing to pay your top people, rest assured someone else will.

13. Organizational hubris. Some organizations think they are good enough to overcome the loss of talented people and top producers. "No big deal. We've lost people before." Sadly, they will soon learn otherwise.

Make sure you study this process and its application to your organization. You don't have to lose your top people.

URIAH THE HITTITE

Embedded in the five verses at the start of this chapter is a dominant theme of loyalty. I would be remiss if I did not close out this chapter without addressing its importance. Loyalty, in and of itself, does not make you a leader. However, disloyalty disqualifies you from leadership positions. Loyalty is a prerequisite if you wish to become mighty and move from pandemic to progress.

Josheb-basshebeth, Eleazar, and Shammah loved David and were deeply loyal to him. They were so loyal that they risked their very lives to bless and refresh him. But what about David? David was obviously loyal as well, or these three would not have been so dedicated to him. However, there was a period of time in David's life when his men were more loyal to him than he was to them.

Chapter 23 concludes by listing the names of all thirty-seven Mighty Men. The last name recorded is Uriah the Hittite. Uriah is an individual everyone should know about because his story has incredible meaning to us.

The name Uriah means "Yahweh is my light." In other words, God directed the attitudes and actions of this mighty warrior. This was unusual at the time because the Hittites were largely a Gentile people antagonistic toward the God of the Jews, the one true God, Jehovah. Uriah, however, was loyal to Yahweh. The one true God had preeminence in his life.

In 2 Samuel 11, we also learn Uriah was married to a breathtakingly beautiful woman named Bathsheba. As recorded in verses 2 through 5 of that chapter, while Uriah was at war, David noticed Bathsheba bathing. Overcome with lust, he ordered for her to be brought to him. Yes, David used his authority to summons a beautiful woman for his personal pleasure. As a result, he did something out of character and slept with the wife of one of his Mighty Men. I can only imagine the guilt, shame, embarrassment, and panic he felt when Bathsheba came to him shortly thereafter and said in verse 5, "I am pregnant."

In an attempt to cover up his sin, David then summoned Uriah from the battlefield to get a "report" on how the war was going. It was David's plan for Uriah to sleep with his wife while back in the city and then pass the pregnancy off as his. But David did not count on the character of Uriah and the loyalty he had to his men.

Uriah said in verse 11, "The ark and Israel and Judah dwell in booths, and my lord Joab and the servants of my lord are camping in the open field. Shall I then go to my house, to eat and to drink and to lie with my wife? As you live, and as your soul lives, I will not do this thing." There was no chance Uriah was going to enjoy all the comforts of home while his men were risking their lives on the battlefield. Uriah was more loyal to his teammates than David was to his.

Ultimately, David sank even deeper into sin and placed Uriah on the front lines of battle, knowing he would die in the heavy fighting. This was later confirmed when a messenger returned from the battlefield and in verses 23 and 24 told David, "The men gained an advantage over us and came out against us in the field, but we drove them back to the entrance of the gate. Then the archers shot at your servants from the wall. Some of the king's servants are dead, and your servant Uriah the Hittite is dead also."

David was a great leader but had some well-known moments of glaring imperfection. This was one of those. There will be times in your leadership when members of your team are not loyal to you. There may be backstabbing, lies, slander, and even attempted coupes from those you have influence over and put great trust in. But as the leader, you must always lead with loyalty. Will you be occasionally hurt and blindsided? Absolutely. But the payoff will be so much greater than the pain you experience because of the depth of meaningful relationships you will build with your own group of mighty men.

David's character and loyalty did not determine Uriah's. And one person's character and loyalty should not determine yours.

CHAPTER 4 STUDY AND DISCUSSION QUESTIONS

Culture is who you hire. Do you have a standardized system for the type of individuals you wish to add to your team? If so, can you spell it out?

_____

_____

_____

Do you currently or have you ever worked for a toxic boss? If so, what were some of the conditions that made your environment so unhealthy?

_____

_____

_____

How often are you, as the leader, among your people? Should you be with them more often? What is the impact when you spend time personally investing in those you lead?

_____

_____

_____

Have you identified the top producers on your team? What are you doing to keep them in the fold?

_____

_____

_____

Are you more loyal to your team or are they more loyal to you? What evidence would you give for your answer? Would your team say the same thing?

_____

_____

_____

CHAPTER 5

Contentment

> *"Now Abishai, the brother of Joab, the son of Zeruiah, was chief of the thirty. And he wielded his spear against three hundred men and killed them and won a name beside the three. He was the most renowned of the thirty and became their commander, but he did not attain to the three."*
>
> —2 Samuel 23:18–19 (ESV)

Abishai fascinates me. Here's what we know about him from the two verses above. He was a brother and son. Abishai was a skilled as a warrior. Much like Josheb-basshebeth, he was proficient at the use of a spear, demonstrated by killing three hundred men during one conflict. Abishai's military credentials were so impressive the text says, "He was the most renowned of the thirty and became their commander."

But this is where his resume becomes so intriguing. The text also says he "won a name beside the three." "The three" were Josheb-basshebeth, Eleazar, and Shammah. But the text goes on to say, "he did not attain to the three."

Every leader of an organization has an inner-circle. These are true influencers of the organization. They are the ones who have the "meetings before the meeting" and the "meetings after the meeting." Other people provide input and give advice. They make decisions.

I have been part of organizations where I have been one of "the three." Conversely, I have been part of organizations where regardless of what I've done, I "did not attain to the three." Part of me thinks Abishai would think and say, "What do I have to do? I mean I've killed three hundred men with a spear. I'm the most renowned soldier of this elite group. In fact, I'm their commander. Tell me, what do I have to do?" I can relate. There have been times I've killed my proverbial three hundred and led my elite forces, yet could not attain the inner-circle status of "the three." Once again, many leaders want influence, not titles.

But that's how I would probably respond. You likely might as well. But Abishai did not, and that's what makes him so compelling. From Abishai, we learn that to become mighty and move from pandemic to progress, you need contentment.

Contentment is a sense of peace, satisfaction, and joy with where you are in your life and leadership. It doesn't mean you have abandoned ambition, personal growth, and self-improvement. It just means you know who you are, and there is a quiet satisfaction during this stage of your journey. You are not defined by others or their expectations. You're comfortable in your own skin. A content person will strive to be the absolute best he or she can be and live with the results. Content people know when God is ready, He will elevate them.

I experienced a masterclass in contentment, preparing for my daughter Anna's wedding. Our family was in full wedding-planning mode. One day, I joined my wife Sonya, in-laws Doug and Barbara Lilley whom this book is dedicated to, and a wonderful saleslady named Lisa at the local Macy's to pick out my suit for the upcoming ceremony.

I'm not a big fan of shopping. I could name countless other things I would rather do than spend time in a mall, picking out clothes. Despite this, I was doing pretty well until it came time to purchase two neckties to go with my suit. I was perplexed for two primary reasons—first, why *two* neckties and not just one? Second, what about all the neckties I never wear hanging in my closet?

Oh well, as my wife, mother-in-law, and Lisa were going through the seemingly endless options of which neckties would look great with my suit, I finally asked, "Can I have a vote?" My wife and mother-in-law simply carried on as if I said nothing. At least Lisa smiled and pleasantly said, "No." I then discovered I was not one of "the three." "The three" were my wife Sonya, my mother-in-law Mrs. Lilley, and Lisa.

It was at that moment I learned three signs of a leader who is not in charge (even if they think they are) and needs to learn to be content.

First, a leader is not in charge when they lack influence on a particular topic. I may have a certain level of positional authority in our family, though I always defer to my father-in-law as my elder and the family's patriarch, but I quickly realized I had no influence on any decisions being made. My fashion sense begins and ends with basic colors, designs, and styles. Rarely will you see me in anything other than workout clothes or blue jeans with a collared shirt. Being fitted for a suit and picking out something "which will not clash with the boutonniere" is clearly outside my comfort zone, and everyone knew it.

Second, you are not in charge when you have little to no subject matter knowledge. During the entire process, I continually deferred to Lisa. With every word and suggestion, you could tell she was making the wedding a better experience for us. Lisa was clearly an expert on men's fashion. I went with every suggestion she made. Few things erode people's confidence in a leader more than when the leader persists in speaking into a topic of which they have little knowledge of while those on their team are subject-matter experts. Simply put, they don't know what they are talking about. That leader needs the contentment and humility to step aside, delegate, and then trust those on their team who are smarter on the topic than they are.

Finally, you are not in charge when you have little to no perspective. Leaders need to develop the ability to intuitively understand how to bring the most value to whatever room they may be in. Because of my lack of influence and subject-matter knowledge of wedding apparel, I needed to understand my highest and best use was to be content, stand quietly off to the side, not cause trouble, and eventually pay the bill. As professional wrestler The Rock used to say, "You need to know your role and shut your mouth!"

Before entering any meeting or engaging in any conversation, leaders should always predetermine where they can add the most value and leverage their influence in those areas. Be content enough to make everyone else as successful as possible. For me, that meant being a good team player and funding the operation. My opinions were not needed or wanted. For you, it may mean something different, but you still need to be humble and content enough to understand when you are not in charge.

Just as you need to learn to be content in certain family dynamics, you need to learn contentment in your career. That's what Abishai did. He was a professional soldier. Yet, he found joy in being a commander who was not one of "the three." Once again, I can relate.

On August 26, 2022, I celebrated twenty years serving pastors, church leaders, and marketplace leaders with INJOY Stewardship Solutions. But there was a fifteen-month period of time during this tenure when I worked for another like-minded organization. During that time, I learned a lot, developed a life-long friendship, helped countless leaders, and developed skills I still use to this day.

But there were many other things, which were a struggle. No matter what position you hold, there are many non-obvious things you must learn at a new job. Non-obvious things are just that—non-obvious.

They are the little things, which will determine your level of influence. Some of the which were the following for me:

- New personalities.
- Body language.
- What people enjoy talking about versus what makes them glaze over or roll their eyes.
- What people celebrate versus what they don't.
- Who are the influencers?
- Do you have any influence?
- How coaching and feedback are delivered—if at all.
- Other than KPIs, how to know if you are doing a good job or not.
- What is in place at your new organization to make you successful.
- What questions are considered good questions versus "Are you kidding me? Can you believe he asked that?"
- What is considered initiative versus assumptive and "That's not how we do things around here."
- Who is insecure versus who really wants your fresh thoughts and perspectives.

Even for the most experienced individuals, it takes a high level of emotional intelligence to navigate new employment opportunities.

THE SHAUN WRIGHT-PHILLIPS SYNDROME

It is often said the grass is not always greener on the other side. The truth is, you may actually have a good thing going right where you currently are. To prove my point, allow me to introduce you to former English footballer Shaun Wright-Phillips and a malady called The Shaun Wright-Phillips Syndrome named after him.

Wright-Phillips showed tremendous potential in his teens and early-twenties, playing for Manchester City. In fact, Wright-Phillips was so talented he won four consecutive Manchester City's Young Player of the Year awards from 2000 to 2003. Wright-Phillips came up through the organization. He was in an environment where he was cared for, brought out the best in him, was committed to his success, and allowed him to perform at his highest level. There was mutual investment there. Wright-Phillips was so happy at Manchester City, he indicated he would never leave. But then money and "opportunity" came calling.

In 2005, Wright-Phillips signed a big-money contract with Chelsea. It was then his career took a sharp downturn. Wright-Phillips was highly compensated but did not have the organizational support system he needed to be successful. Within three years, Wright-Phillips had fallen out of favor with the club and its manager. He was then allowed to leave the squad. Wright-Phillips would have been better off making less money but remaining in a more ideal culture for him.

No job is perfect, but if you are in a situation where you are successful and systems are in place to ensure your ongoing success, be very, very careful about leaving it for more money or "opportunity." You may receive increased income, but over time your influence will be dramatically reduced. It will not be worth it. Frustration and failure will be your constant companions. If this happens, you have become a victim of the Shaun Wright-Phillips Syndrome. To become mighty and move from pandemic to progress, be content to chase culture instead of money.

Leaders must also be content with their decision-making. Just as important if not more so, they must be equally content knowing when those decisions need to be changed for the good of their organizations.

Twenty years ago, I was sitting in our company president's office. He was wanting to make changes to a recently implemented major marketing initiative, and I mentioned to him there would be pushback from the team. When he asked why, I said, "Well, they will say, 'That's not what he said last week.'" Candidly, I did not tell him this, but was I thinking the same thing myself.

After an uncomfortable moment of silence, he leaned forward, sternly looked at me in the eye and said, "Brian, maybe I have different information than I had last week. Maybe I've (personally) grown in the last week. Maybe I have had some new thoughts, new ideas. Maybe the market has changed. Maybe our skill set as team has improved. Brian, maybe I'm a better leader today than I was last week. That is why maybe I see things differently from time to time. Don't you?"

Now came the teaching moment. He concluded by saying, "Brian, never be afraid of the phrase 'That's not what you said last week.' Just make sure you can communicate that things are different, you are different, and why new approaches are now required based upon this new information."

COACH BRUCE ARIANS

On January 2, 2022, Tampa Bay Buccaneers wide receiver Antonio Brown shockingly took his pads off during the middle of a game, and the shirtless player simply walked off the field. Brown, who had a long history of questionable behavior, had been given a chance at redemption by the club and head coach Bruce Arians. Arians was later questioned by the media as to why he gave the troubled wide receiver multiple chances to improve his behavior after saying the previous year he would cut him if he made one mistake.

Similar to my previous company president, Arians answered, "The history has changed since that statement. A lot of things went on last year that I was very proud of him, and I made a decision that this was the best thing for our football team." When the reporter asked a follow-up question about what people would think of his decision, Arians colorfully said, "I could give a s*#t what they think. The only thing I care about is this football team and what's best for us."

Leaders, you will always be questioned. It is part of leadership. If you are not mentally or emotionally prepared for regular cross-examination, you may want to forego potential leadership responsibilities. You never want to be reckless, indecisive, or unsure of your decisions. But never, ever, be afraid of the phrase "That's not what you said last week" if you have new and better information.

COACH LARRY BROWN

Few people have the resume of Larry Brown. While at the University of North Carolina from 1960–1963, he played college basketball for Hall of Fame coaches Frank McGuire and Dean Smith. He then won a gold medal in the 1964 Olympics under another Hall of Fame coach Hank Iba.

Though he was a three-time all-star as a professional player, it quickly became apparent Brown was a natural at coaching. Over the course of twenty-seven seasons, he would amass a 1,275–965 lifetime record while leading eight different ABA and NBA teams to the play-offs. In addition, Brown won an additional 262 games coaching the UCLA Bruins, Kansas Jayhawks, and SMU Mustangs at the collegiate level.

Brown is the only head coach to win both the NCAA and NBA championships, leading Kansas and the Detroit Pistons respectively to titles. In 2002, he was inducted into the Basketball Hall of Fame. In 2021, Brown was awarded the Chuck Daly Lifetime Achievement Award by National Basketball Coaches Association.

If anyone had the right to say, "I know everything there is to know about the game of basketball and coaching," it would be Larry Brown.

With his experience as a gold medal-winning player, a championship coach on multiple levels, and a Hall of Fame career, he has seen and done it all. But Brown takes the exact opposite approach. He humbly takes on the posture of a continual learner.

Because of Brown's vast knowledge, he is frequently asked to observe numerous teams' practices throughout the year and give his feedback. While he is there to advise and impart wisdom, it is actually Brown who always learns something new.

The following are five practical things you can do to become a continual learner like Coach Brown:

First, read books. Books expose you to the thoughts and experiences of people you will probably never meet. Also, you are likely facing problems today, which have already been solved by others. Their answers are only a few click away on Amazon or Barnes & Noble. Second, travel. The world is a *very* big place. Traveling expands your perspective and knowledge of what is possible.

Third, listen. When you are talking, you are sharing what you know. When you actively listen, you learn what others know. Fourth, ask great questions. Be curious. Be humble. Be content, knowing you don't know everything and there is something you can learn from anyone. A side benefit of this is interested people are always more interesting themselves.

Finally, hang around people smarter and more experienced than you are. They are an endless wealth of knowledge. If Coach Larry Brown can still be learning new things every day, so can we.

WILL SMITH AND THE SLAP HEARD AROUND THE WORLD

Someone who learned quite a bit about himself and the consequences of their decisions was Will Smith. During the 2022 Oscars ceremony, Smith and Chris Rock were part of one of the most uncomfortable, disturbing, infamous, and most talked-about moments ever witnessed in television history.

As is the tradition in these type of events, Rock was roasting many of the members of the audience. This happens annually at the Oscars, Golden Globes, ESPYs, Grammys, and other awards shows. But Rock's statement to Smith's wife, Jada Pinkett-Smith, apparently crossed a line when he said, "*G.I. Jane 2*, can't wait to see it."

Will Smith initially laughed at the joke but then came on stage and slapped Rock in the face. For those who do not know, Smith's wife suffers from alopecia, an autoimmune condition causing hair loss. Afterward, from his seat in the first row, Smith twice shouted, "Keep my wife's name out of your [expletive] mouth." The audience was stunned. Twitter exploded. The issue has since been examined from every possible angle.

I will now give my thoughts. At the time of this writing, we currently live in a lawless land. Will Smith should have been arrested. Period. Assault is generally defined as "intentionally putting another person in reasonable apprehension of an imminent harmful or offensive contact. Physical injury is not required." Notice the legal definition does not state anything about whether the act was justified or not. Smith's slap obviously would classify as offensive contact and put Rock in a reasonable apprehension of harmful contact.

I am still confused as to why Smith was allowed to return to his seat and less than an hour later, win an award, get a standing ovation, and then say, "I'm being called on in my life to love people and to protect people. And to be a river to my people." This action would indicate Smith's river is polluted with hypocrisy and lawlessness.

It is confusing as to what Smith was expecting. He was the presumptive winner of Best Actor for his portrayal of Richard Williams in the film *King Richard*. Smith was seated in the front row. Once again, comedians with a history of roasting people were often employed to be the show's hosts. Traditionally, "poking fun" at the stars is what happens at these events. The Smiths should have been content in first, who they are, and second, the environment in which they were in.

But we were also reminded of a basic form of respect and human decency which is to never have fun at someone else's expense. Dignity is the imprint of God on every human soul. "I was just kidding" is never an excuse for degrading comments. Degrading a person and hurting their feelings for the purposes of increasing our own self-worth, entertainment, or public standing is unadvisable and just plain wrong. Maybe this will be the beginning of the ending of "roasting" people and the start of celebrating them instead.

What was also evident is angry people become foolish people. The only difference between anger and danger is a "D." Since Smith inserted God into his acceptance speech by saying, "I am overwhelmed by what God is calling on me to do and be in this world," allow me to share with you what God actually says about angry people. I could have listed dozens and dozens more verses but will stop with this group of fifteen.

1. "Therefore, having put away falsehood, let each one of you speak the truth with his neighbor, for we are members one of another. Be angry and do not sin; do not let the sun go down on your anger, and give no opportunity to the devil"—Ephesians 4:25–27 (ESV).

2. "Know this, my beloved brothers: let every person be quick to hear, slow to speak, slow to anger; for the anger of man does not produce the righteousness of God"—James 1:19–20 (ESV).

3. "A fool gives full vent to his spirit, but a wise man quietly holds it back"—Proverbs 29:11 (ESV).

4. "A gentle answer turns away wrath, but a harsh word stirs up anger"—Proverbs 15:1 (NIV).

5. "Whoever is patient has great understanding, but one who is quick-tempered displays folly"—Proverbs 14:29 (NIV).

6. "Fools give full vent to their rage, but the wise bring calm in the end"—Proverbs 29:11 (NIV).

7. "Fools show their annoyance at once, but the prudent overlook an insult"—Proverbs 12:16 (NIV).

8. "It is to one's honor to avoid strife, but every fool is quick to quarrel"—Proverbs 20:3 (NIV).

9. "The discretion of a man deferreth his anger; and it is his glory to pass over a transgression"—Proverbs 19:11 (KJV).

10. "An angry man stirreth up strife, and a furious man aboundeth in transgression"—Proverbs 29:22 (KJV).

11. "Be not hasty in thy spirit to be angry: for anger resteth in the bosom of fools"—Ecclesiastes 7:9 (KJV).

12. "Be not overcome of evil, but overcome evil with good"—Romans 12:21 (KJV).

13. "Let all bitterness, and wrath, and anger, and clamour, and evil speaking, be put away from you, with all malice" —Ephesians 4:31 (KJV).

14. "A wrathful man stirreth up strife: but he that is slow to anger appeaseth strife" —Proverbs 15:18 (KJV).

15. "Make no friendship with an angry man; and with a furious man thou shalt not go" —Proverbs 22:24 (KJV).

From a biblical perspective derived from the previous verses, Smith's actions were dangerous, devilish, unrighteous, foolish, unwise, harsh, lacking understanding and discretion, unhinged, furious, hasty, bitter, wrathful, toxic, violent, and just evil. Once again, "let every person be quick to hear, slow to speak, slow to anger; for the anger of man does not produce the righteousness of God."

Anger also makes the other person the victim. I have lost my temper on multiple occasions. Each time, I ended up looking bad, and the object of my anger was viewed as a victim. Once again, it did not matter if my anger was justified. I made the other person the sympathetic figure as I came across unhinged and lacking self-control, much like Will Smith.

Chris Rock took the high road as Smith's behavior sadly overshadowed the defining moment of his acting career. One thing I am sure of is, Smith deeply regrets walking on the stage and slapping Rock.

Finally, one of the problems in our world today is the lack of statesmen. Statesmen are dignified individuals who are respected and have morale authority. Statesmen are E.F. Huttons—when they speak everyone listens. They are above the fray. However, in the midst of this chaos and confusion, a statesman stood up on the Hollywood floor and brought a sense of peace and calm to all the chaos.

Denzel Washington, noted Christian and acting legend, told Smith, "At your highest moment, be careful. That's when the devil comes for you." Peter Etenung tweeted, "I refuse to behave like Will Smith. I refuse to behave like Chris Rock. I prefer to behave like Denzel Washington. In a very uncomfortable and heated moment, he gave wisdom, understanding, correction and comfort." Etenung's words provide for us the four defining characteristics of Statesmen—wisdom, understanding, correction, and comfort. May I also add statesmen are content.

Everyone reading this page is now faced with a choice. Your circumstances do not affect your decisions. You can either be a statesman who rises above the fray like Denzel Washington, or you can be angry person who acts foolishly like Will Smith. You decide.

COACH BILL SELF

One leader who did behave admirably in adverse circumstances was Kansas Jayhawks head basketball coach Bill Self. The Jayhawks trailed the North Carolina Tar Heels by fifteen points, 40–25 at halftime of the 2022 NCAA men's college basketball championship game. Coach Self could have addressed the team's poor first-half performance in a number of ways. For instance, he could have kicked over the water cooler and broke a blackboard like you often see in movies or hear about. Or, Coach Self could have been solemn and expressed disappointment over the team missing a once-in-a-lifetime opportunity.

Perhaps he could have been gentle while reminding the team of what a great year it had been and how proud he was of them. Coach Self could have even been passive and simply delegated to the assistant coaches the task of communicating halftime adjustments. But he chose another path.

Coach Self said, "I didn't say much. I told them at half, 'Would you be rather down fifteen with twenty minutes left or down nine with two minutes left?' They said, 'Let's take fifteen.' They played off that." The Jayhawks then proceeded to outscore the Tar Heels 20–6 to start the second half and would go on to win the game 72–69. Coach Self had given the team the right words at the right time. Leaders can learn several lessons from Coach Self's halftime speech:

Leaders must remain positive at all times, but especially during crisis. This does not mean you should not properly evaluate reality, but Coach Self was calm in the midst of his circumstances. There was a sense of peace and contentment. He knew there was still time left to win the game if the Jayhawks did the things necessary to do so.

Leaders must also provide hope and point to a brighter tomorrow. Coach Self was providing hope and let his players know there was still a chance for victory. This was possible because Coach Self believed in his team. His speech was not patronizing or full of empty promises. Because he knew how much work they had put in, how they played throughout the year, and what type of young men they were, they still had a chance for victory.

Finally, leaders must reframe adversity. Michael Lombardi of *The Daily Coach* wrote, "Self's team wasn't happy at the half, and by contextualizing the problem, he persuaded his players to overcome adversity and eliminate their mistakes."

You see, being content is always a smart strategy because things can always get worse. This is what Self was saying. I'm paraphrasing, but what he told his team was, "Hey, we're down by fifteen with twenty minutes to go. But would you rather have that or be down nine with two minutes to go? OK then, it could be worse. Let's go!" Once again, I'm paraphrasing, but you get the point.

There are leaders reading these words today who need to reframe the adversity they are currently facing. Yes, there is still much work to be done and issues to be addressed. But it could be worse.

If you are facing significant hardship as an organization, remain positive, provide hope, believe in your people, and reframe adversity. By doing so, you will give your team a chance to reverse negative momentum and achieve all your desired goals.

COACH JURGEN KLOPP

Coach Self is not the only manager whose halftime approach changed the fortunes of their team. Even the most successful organizations lose focus and momentum from time to time. It is during these moments of stagnation and poor performance when great leaders shine the brightest. Such a moment took place on May 4, 2022. The Liverpool football club trailed Villarreal 2–0 at halftime. The team's incomparable manager Jurgen Klopp knew he needed to do something to help the team regain focus and lost momentum.

Klopp is someone who leads from a place of contentment and positivity. He traditionally begins halftime speeches with highlights of the team's best plays from the first half, reinforcing positive behaviors. But there was little to get excited about in this game. No video would be shown. The team was sloppy, lacked composure, and made too many errors.

As reported by *The Athletic*'s James Pearce, Klopp then used motivational words and tactical changes to inspire his team. The players responded by going on to a 3–2 victory. So what did Klopp say and do that caused the team to reverse its fortunes? His actions provide a template for any leader facing similar circumstances.

First, just like Coach Self, Klopp remained calm. He did not panic or overreact. Instead, Klopp provided hope. He reminded his team that a tie was still very much in the team's reach. He actually underestimated what his team would do.

Second, he got back to the basics. When tough times come, get back to what you do best. Return to the fundamentals. Klopp told the team, "Play football, play the Liverpool way—how we've played all season." He added the team needed to be "brave, stronger and move smarter ... change the momentum."

Third, focus on getting small wins under your belt. Every great journey starts with a single step. Klopp advised his team to just focus on getting the next goal. The first step in regaining lost momentum is to focus on getting one small win. Then another. Then another.

Finally, Klopp made tactical adjustments. Yes, you need to get back to the basics but "new" generates momentum. If you keep doing what you've been doing, you'll keep getting what you've been getting. The team was trailing and adjustments were desperately needed. Klopp said, "We couldn't find the midfielders in the half-space because they were not there and the front three were too fixed. There was no flexibility, so we had to mix it up to cause them more problems." And mix it up Klopp did. There are probably a number of leaders reading this right now who need to mix some things up as well.

What were the results of Jurgen Klopp remaining calm and content, getting back to the basics, focusing on getting small wins, and making tactical adjustments? His team scored three goals in twelve minutes and won the match. That's progress. The same could happen for you.

WALTER ORTHMANN

Even if your names are Bill Self or Jurgen Klopp, all leadership is temporary. No matter how important you are, someone will eventually be filling your seat. As a result, we are all interim leaders; however Walter Orthmann from Brazil recently challenged this long-held leadership belief.

The May 5, 2022 edition of *Morning Brew* told the story of Orthmann. What is extraordinary about this man is he is 100 years old and had an eighty-four-year tenure at Industrias Renaux S.A. Orthmann, who holds the Guinness World Record for the longest career with a single company, finally retired as the company's sales manager. He had started as a shipping assistant in 1938 at fifteen years of age. To give you some sense of how long ago 1938 was, the following are some of the notable things which happened that year:

- The March of Dimes was founded.
- Mass panic broke out in the Eastern United States as Orson Welles performed his *War of the Worlds* radio broadcast.
- Nuclear fission was discovered.
- Under Adolf Hitler's direction, Germany invaded Poland.
- Germany began its persecution of the Jewish people.
- *Action Comics #1* was published with the first appearance of Superman.
- The ballpoint pen was invented.
- Jimmie Fox won the MLB Most Valuable Player Award.
- And Walter Orthmann went to work for Industrias Renaux S.A.

What was the secret to his longevity? Obviously, he possessed uncommon contentment, people skills, the ability to change, and the occupational stamina to consistently hit goals and objectives over an extended period of time. According to the *Morning Brew* e-newsletter, Orthmann said, "I don't do much planning, nor care much about tomorrow. All I care about is that tomorrow will be another day in which I will wake up, get up, exercise, and go to work; you need to get busy with the present, not the past or the future. Here and now is what counts. So, let's go to work!"

Perhaps the secret to longevity is not as complex as we would like to think. Maybe the secret to longevity is being content, developing a short-term memory, and the ability to stay in the moment, focusing on the here and now.

New England Patriots head coach Bill Belichick was once asked in a news conference, "With all that you have accomplished in your career, what are some of the things left you still want to accomplish?" Belichick answered, "I'd like to go out and have a good practice today. That would be on the list right now." Belichick is the embodiment of staying in the moment and focusing on the present.

High-performance expert Alan Stein Jr. quoted mental skills coach Graham Betchart in his book *Sustain Your Game: High Performance Keys to Manage Stress, Avoid Stagnation, and Beat Burnout*, "Great players, he explained, let go of the play that just happened and never worry about what might happen; they simply focus on what is." Be content. Focus. It is today that matters, not yesterday nor tomorrow.

Father Time is still undefeated, but Walter Orthmann has taken him into multiple overtimes. For eighty-four years he focused on waking up, getting up, exercising, and going to work, and did so with a historic level of success. Maybe we should follow his example.

BEES ARE ACTUALLY FISH

You must be comfortable with who you are if you want to be content. On May 31, 2022, a surprising ruling came down from the State of

California Third Appellate District. In the case of *Almond Alliance of California v. Fish And Game Commission*, the court ruled that bees could be officially classified as fish. Here's the backstory on what appears impossible to believe.

In 2018, four different species of California bees were in danger of becoming extinct. Several groups began petitioning for their protection. The court then ruled these particular bees were an endangered species. Their thought was Section 45 of the California Fish and Game Code defined fish as "a wild fish, mollusk, crustacean, invertebrate, amphibian, or part, spawn, or ovum of any of those animals." As you can see, most of what is listed, the normal person would not classify as fish. Therefore, a loophole existed to lump the endangered bees into this group as well.

Bottom line—the California Court of Appeals now says bees are fish.

What does this have to do with leadership? Ironically, it has everything to do with leadership. Leaders cannot take their organizations and teams from Point A to Point B without first knowing where Point A actually is. As a result, the first and primary responsibility of leadership is to properly define reality. You cannot effectively move forward otherwise.

Leaders have a responsibility to properly assess the following areas of their responsibilities:

- Current Culture
- Strengths
- Weaknesses
- Marketplace Opportunities
- Threats
- Financial Position
- Employee Performance
- Spiritual Condition

- The Future
- Leadership Pipeline
- Physical Health
- State of Your Personal and Professional Relationships

The California Court of Appeals appear to have a problem telling the difference between a bee and a fish. They apparently have a problem defining reality. In fact, they are distorting reality to fit their agenda. May we not do the same. May we be content with who and what we are. What we are called to do as leaders is too important to do otherwise.

JURASSIC PARK

Someone who knows exactly who they are and what their brand is are the makers of the *Jurassic Park* franchise. More importantly, they know their audience. The *Jurassic Park* movies are built around a simple premise—dinosaurs chasing people, eating an unfortunate group of them, and scaring us in the process as they do it. The film's producers are not trying to win an Academy Award unless it's for special effects and sound. As a leader, don't try to be something you're not. Be content with who you are. Play to your strengths. Give the audience what they want. And when you do, you will reap the benefits of this approach. The makers of the *Jurassic Park* franchise have made over $6 billion in worldwide revenues.

I do not want to confuse contentment with comfort. A common leadership axiom is leaders must become comfortable being uncomfortable. What this means is growth happens when you stretch beyond your comfort zone. I and other successful leaders agree. Being uncomfortable is where you learn new things, have new thoughts, meet new people, and have new experiences. Uncomfortable leaders have the chance to become stronger, smarter, more experienced, and more talented.

Unfortunately, this is not the default mode for most leaders. Most leaders default to comfort, not discomfort. Becoming uncomfortable is a choice. It is a mindset. And those who make the choice to embrace being uncomfortable often rise to the top of their professions.

COACH NICK SABAN

One such leader is someone we've talked a lot about, Alabama Crimson Tide head football coach Nick Saban. One of the best chapters in John Talty's book *The Leadership Secrets of Nick Saban: How Alabama's Coach Became the Greatest Ever* focuses on Coach Saban's use of "distressed assets." These "assets" are former head coaches, fired in fact, whom he employs as analysts to assist the program. Some of these analysts have included Butch Jones, Al Groh, Billy Napier, Bill O'Brien, and Steve Sarkisian. Most programs considered these individuals less than desirable or even toxic. But Coach Saban was willing to take a chance on them because of Alabama's healthy culture. They also possessed certain skills, which could help the program at an inexpensive rate.

Many leaders would be insecure bringing in a group of high-profile, high-capacity leaders. After all, how many of those "distressed assets" might be Trojan Horses who would eventually want his job. They could divide allegiances, undermine authority, take credit for successes, and think they could do the job better than the leader could. The insecurity this could breed is why so many leaders only surround themselves with people less talented than they are. But not Coach Saban.

Talty writes, "Saban was willing to think outside the box and hire the most veteran graduate assistant he'd ever had in Groh. That one hire forever changed how organizations looked at their off-field hires and highlighted what was possible when you strived to be better rather than to be comfortable."

Those words about Coach Saban should challenge all comfortable leaders. To find out if you are such a leader, the following are ten signs you have become too comfortable:

1. You only surround yourself with people less talented than you.

2. You use yesterday's solutions in an attempt to solve today's problems. You are an expert in what used to work.

3. You avoid all forms of conflict, which might challenge you and move the organization forward.

4. You haven't read a new book in months—or even years. Let's be honest, if you're reading this page, this does not describe you. But this is something to challenge others with.

5. All of your stories are from many years ago. You continually talk about the "good old days" rather than what is coming up.

6. If you do public speaking, you continually recycle old content.

7. You never visit anywhere new. There are no new experiences. "Been there, done that" is your motto.

8. The status quo is just fine for you. In fact, now you even consider average to be deemed as excellence.

9. You rationalize not hitting goals.

10. You no longer have big dreams. Your best days are in the past. You're now in maintenance mode, just passing time and riding out the clock.

You do not want to be a comfortable leader. No one wants to follow comfortable leaders. Comfortable leaders cause stagnation in the organization and frustration in its people.

Follow Coach Saban's example instead. Think outside the box, continually look for competitive advantages, surround yourself with as many smart and talented people as possible, keep focusing on tomorrow, and always feel the best is yet to come. This mindset will prevent you from becoming too comfortable as a leader. No one wants to follow comfortable leaders. But people will line up to follow content leaders who are mighty and take people from pandemic to progress.

So how do you handle someone who is discontented? Perhaps someone on your team has been impatient or overestimated their skills and approached you asking, "Why don't you let me lead?" This is a cringeworthy statement because leadership is earned, never given.

As you know by now, leadership is influence, not position. Positions can be assigned or given. Influence, on the other hand, is only earned by effectively serving others. Your presence, communication skills, sense of authority, expertise, and courage allow you the opportunity to assume the mantle of leadership. Let's look at each of those terms I just mentioned.

- Presence—One thing I continually trumpet is leadership happens among the people and not in the corner office or green room. Servant leadership should be your brand. You should be the first to arrive and the last to leave. You should both weep and celebrate with your team. The shepherd should smell like the sheep.

- Communication Skills—There comes a time during every leader's tenure when they must stand up and say, "This is where we are going. Follow me!" Therefore, effective communication skills are a must.

- Sense of Authority—There is a sense of gravitas to leaders who are worth following. We get the word *gravity* from gravitas. There is weightiness to what the leader says and does. When the leader speaks, you listen because you know they know what they are talking about. There is credibility there.

- Expertise—Effective leadership knows what it is doing. People will not follow a leader who does not know where they are going or how to get there even if they did. An incompetent leader is a short-term positional leader.

- Courage—Leaders must continually advance the mission and vision of the organization in the midst of opposition and uncertainty.

Leadership is not an announcement or a position. It is a direction. So when someone wonders why they were passed over for leadership opportunities, talk to them about their presence, communication skills, courage, sense of authority, and expertise. And then develop a plan to help them improve.

CHAPTER 5 STUDY AND DISCUSSION QUESTIONS

Are you comfortable celebrating the success of others?

_____

_____

_____

When a crisis hits, how do you react? Do you remain calm or does your personality escalate to an unhealthy level?

_____

_____

_____

Would others describe you as a person with anger issues? What evidence would they give for their answer?

_____

_____

_____

Can you properly evaluate reality as a leader? If so, what is the current reality of your organization? Would those on your team agree with you?

_____

_____

_____

Other than *Mighty*, what was the last book you read? What did you learn from it? How are your applying it?

_____

_____

_____

CHAPTER 6

Courage

And Benaiah the son of Jehoiada was a valiant man of Kabzeel, a doer of great deeds. He struck down two ariels of Moab. He also went down and struck down a lion in a pit on a day when snow had fallen. And he struck down an Egyptian, a handsome man. The Egyptian had a spear in his hand, but Benaiah went down to him with a staff and snatched the spear out of the Egyptian's hand and killed him with his own spear. These things did Benaiah the son of Jehoiada and won a name beside the three mighty men. He was renowned among the thirty, but he did not attain to the three. And David set him over his bodyguard."

—2 Samuel 23: 20–23 (ESV)

The next of the Mighty Men we will look at is Benaiah. He was a valiant man. Benaiah came from Kabzeel which was the most remote city of Judah. He was used to operating in the wilderness. This would help explain how he developed the skills necessary to kill a lion. Much like Abishai, he was an incredible warrior whose exploits are so renowned that they are recorded for all eternity in the Bible, but he also did not attain the level of "the three." However, there are two qualities I see in his life that will help you become mighty and move from pandemic to progress.

First is Benaiah's courage. He slayed two ariels of Moab. The word *ariels* can be translated "lions of God." These were likely men of great valor and stature. Not only did Benaiah kill "lion men," the text records his killing of an actual lion in a pit. Finally, Benaiah was such a mighty warrior that he took a spear from a handsome Egyptian's hand and killed him with his own weapon. Now that's a bad man! Benaiah's skills allowed him to be placed over all of David's bodyguards.

Second, he is a son. Benaiah is the son of Jehoida. With the exception of Josheb-basshebeth, the lineage of the previous men was listed as well. Eleazar was the son of Dodo, Shammah was the son of Agee, and Abishai was the son of Zeruiah. From this, we can discern that to become mighty and move from pandemic to progress, it certainly helps when an engaged father imprints courage on your heart and soul. I'm not saying people from homes with disengaged, abusive, or absentee fathers cannot develop the courage needed to become mighty. What I am saying is it certainly helps.

Before unpacking the subject of courage, let's look at the legacy left by the leader of the Mighty Men himself, David as a father. A previous chapter mentioned Bathsheba gave birth to David's son. In fact, they would ultimately have four sons together. The second son's name was Solomon.

David would eventually leave the wilderness and assume his rightful place as king of Israel. Israel would experience its greatest period of prosperity and military dominance under his reign. King David would grow into an iconic and revered leader, but like all of us, the time of his passing would eventually come. As we mentioned, all leadership is temporary. First Chronicles 28 and 29 tells us the story of his death and transitioning of the nation's leadership to his son Solomon. In these two chapters, this great king gives us a beautiful picture of how a patriarch of a family can imprint courage and leadership on the heart of a son and leave a godly legacy to the next generation.

1. To leave a godly legacy to the next generation you must disciple them. You must instruct and teach them. In 28:9, King David says,

"As for you, my son Solomon, know the God of your father." Leaving a godly legacy means constantly telling the stories of God's goodness and faithfulness in your life. Deuteronomy 6:6–7 says, "And these words that I command you today shall be on your heart. You shall teach them diligently to your children, and shall talk of them when you sit in your house, and when you walk by the way, and when you lie down, and when you rise!"

2. You must encourage them. The next generation is dying for inspiration. In fact, we all are. Too often, older people tell the next generation everything they are doing wrong. King David did otherwise. It says in verse 10, "for the Lord has chosen you to build a house for the sanctuary; be strong and do it."

3. You must equip them. You must give the next generation your plans, expertise, experience and energy. This is what King David does in verses 11 and 12 of chapter 28. It reads:

> Then David gave to his son Solomon the plan of the porch of the temple, its buildings, its storehouses, its upper rooms, and the room for the atoning cover; and the plan of all that he had in mind, for the courtyards of the house of the Lord, and for all the surrounding rooms, for the storehouses of the house of God and for the storehouses of dedicated things.

4. You must supply resources for them. Throughout verses 13–19, King David provides an itemized list of the money and possessions he left for Solomon to complete the temple's construction. He also gives him people to help him, along with their support in verse 21.

5. You must empower them. People are naturally insecure. It is vital they know you support them. King David tells Solomon in verse 20, "Be strong and of good courage, and do it; do not fear nor be

dismayed for the Lord God—my God—will be with you. He will not leave you nor forsake you, until you have finished all the work for the service of the house of the Lord."

6. You must position them for success. With the start of chapter 29, we see King David shifting his communication to the Jewish people. It says in verse 1, "King David said to all the assembly." In addition to giving the next generation plans and resources, you must also give them access to your platform.

7. You must publicly affirm them. Leaving a godly legacy to the next generation means loaning them your influence. Point to them and tell others God's hand is on their life. King David referred to his son as "My son Solomon, whom alone God has chosen."

8. You must remind them there is work left for them to do. Transparency and authenticity are attractive qualities to the next generation. Be honest with them. Struggle is necessary for developing strength. Do not downplay the challenges they will have in the coming days ahead. King David continues, "(Solomon) is young and inexperienced, and the work is great."

9. You must point them to Jesus. King David was about to remind his son all of this wealth was not merely for his personal enjoyment. There must be a higher purpose, a higher calling in mind. He said in verse 1 of chapter 29, "the temple is not for man, but for the Lord God."

10. You must reassure them. It is a humbling and daunting task to be thrust into a significant position of responsibility. But King David reminded Solomon he had been setup for success. The temple's completion was doable. In verses 2 and 3, King David lists everything that had already been prepared. The project was well underway.

11. You must release them. This is the day parents have worked years for but dread to see when it finally comes. The time eventually comes for the next generation to leave home and plant their own stake in the world. In verse 5, King David asks the people, "Who then is willing to consecrate himself this day to the Lord?"

12. You must celebrate with them. Upon releasing them, celebrate their success. After an offering of biblical proportions, verse 9 says, "Then the people rejoiced, for they had offered willingly, because with a loyal heart they had offered willingly to the Lord; and King David also rejoiced greatly." (NASB)

Being a parent is not for the weak at heart. It takes courage. King David left a godly legacy and an imprint on the future we all still benefit from today. You, too, can send people forth into a time we cannot see with positive effects. Which one of those twelve steps can you begin implementing today to better leave a godly legacy?

UKRAINIAN PRESIDENT VOLODYMYR ZELENSKY

King David was an extraordinarily courageous political leader. A modern-day political leader displaying extraordinary courage at the time of this writing is Ukrainian President Volodymyr Zelensky. Because of his bravery and commitment to his nation's people in the face of insurmountable Russian opposition, President Zelensky has inspired the entire world. His steadfastness is evoking memories of Winston Churchill and setting a standard for all future leaders to follow. The prayers of the entire world are continually for God's protection of President Zelensky and the people of Ukraine.

Shortly after the February 24, 2022, invasion of his country, NBC's Erin McLaughlin gave a compelling profile of the Ukrainian leader. Her report painted a beautiful picture of courageous leadership.

President Zelensky's devotion to his country and people has been celebrated across the globe. McLaughlin correctly assessed when she said, "He is being hailed as a hero both at home and abroad for his leadership as Russian troops invade." However, his courage is not without great personal risk. President Zelensky, though, has remained constant in his support of his fellow countrymen. It was noted that "Despite great personal risk, the forty-four-year-old has vowed to remain in Kyiv, refusing to leave his nation and his people behind."

President Zelensky also has shown incredible bravery by confronting the Russian opposition. He has frequently posted videos, asking the Russian forces to leave Ukraine. President Zelensky also demonstrated one of the defining characteristics of great leadership when he provided clarity in the midst of fear and uncertainty. United States president Joe Biden asked Zelensky to evacuate, to which he replied, "The fight is here. I need ammunition, not a ride."

This Churchillian leadership style inspired others to action as well. A thirty-five-year-old Ukranian named Natasha said, "We're still here and inspiring ordinary Ukrainians to join in the fight." She added, "He gives me confidence." Giving others confidence is what great leaders do. As mentioned earlier, they also lead for a time they cannot see. Natasha concluded her comments by saying, "For me, Zelensky is the real fighter for democracy worldwide and for the peaceful future of our children." President Zelensky is also a deeply compassionate leader. A former advisor said he was "saddened by Ukrainian suffering but determined."

President Zelensky is many things. He is a husband, father of two children, and a Jewish leader who is a descendant of Holocaust survivors. But more than anything, he is a picture of the Ukrainian people he has been called to serve. The aforementioned survivor noted, "I think this is the first time in Ukrainian history that we have a truly Ukrainian president. He's a direct reflection of what Ukrainian people are thinking, feeling, and how they are. He's one of us."

McLaughlin concluded her report with the sobering statement, "Russia's main objective is to physically eliminate him and he hasn't left. That tells you what kind of man he is."

UKRAINIAN PARLIAMENT MEMBER KIRA RUDIK

Crisis does not make a leader; it reveals one. Appearing on the February 24, 2022, edition of *The Sean Hannity Show*, Ukrainian Parliament member Kira Rudik discussed the reasons why she chose to arm herself and stay in Kyiv and defend her family, city, and country from the Russian military. Rudik said, "It was own decision to stay here and not to flee. First of all, because I'm a politician and I'm representing my people, and they didn't go anywhere." What an extraordinary statement from an extraordinary leader!

While things appeared in dire straits, Rudik also provided hope for her people and country. She said, "Second, because I woke up, I looked at all of this and was thinking why would we do this? Why would we go away? He's (Russian President Putin) coming to relent with his forces (and) we are able to fight him back. We are actually doing it very good. In two days, he lost like 3,000 men which is probably the most he lost in the latest wars he was fighting throughout the world. So the Ukrainian army is fighting him very, very hard, and we are resisting in the best ways of the Resistance. So I believe we'll be able to fight back."

Notice the phrases she uses:

- "Why would we go away?"
- "We are able to fight him back."
- "We are actually doing it very good."
- "The Ukrainian army is fighting him very, very hard."
- "We are resisting in the best ways."
- "We'll be able to fight back."

May we all be inspired by the leadership of President Zelensky and Parliamentarian Rudik to become the type of leaders they are, ones who courageously stand in the face of opposition, do not retreat, and inspire others to do likewise. Once again, our prayers are for the safety of the Ukrainian people. May God protect them.

BEAR ATTACKS

In addition to military victories, Benaiah also had to have the courage to conquer natural forces as he killed a lion in a snowy pit. Few things are as harrowing as unexpectedly encountering dangerous animals in the wild.

In July 2013, Matt Dyer was hiking with a group of friends in Canada's Torngat Mountains National Park in Newfoundland and Labrador. Matt felt lucky as one afternoon his party was fortunate enough to see a polar bear about 150 yards away, or so they thought. They were not only watching the polar bear, the polar bear was watching them.

As told to Emma Veidt in the January/February 2022 edition of *Backpacker Magazine,* the bear watched the hikers for several hours. Concern was starting to build. As they prepared for bedtime, their guides setup an electric fence around camp for protection. Skeptical about the fence's ability to keep out a polar bear, they were assured that even though it ran on only two Double D batteries, it generated enough power to deter any bears from approaching the camp. Though he was quite anxious, Dyer fell asleep.

At 2:30 a.m., he was awoken by movement outside his tent. As Dyer looked up, he saw a giant shadow in the shape of a bear hovering above his tent. Dyer screamed as the bear pounced down on top of him. It was then his worst fears became reality.

Dyer's head became lodged in the bear's jaws. Holding him by head, the bear began to drag Dyer's helpless body away from the campsite. Feeling his own skull being crushed by the polar bear's jaws, Dyer began thinking he was about to die. Suddenly, the polar bear was shot by a fellow hiker's flare gun causing it to release Dyer. After initially scampering away, the bear returned to finish him off. Fortunately, the bear was shot again, stopping a subsequent attack.

With the electric fence now destroyed, Dyer's fellow hikers stood guard with their flare guns for the next eight hours, waiting on a rescue helicopter to arrive. Though Dyer had a cracked jaw, several cracked vertebrae, multiple gashes, a punctured lung, and a busted larynx among other injuries, he was alive and would survive.

Whatever you are facing as you read this book, however big or small it may be, your level of expectation will determine your level of preparation. Many of us are approaching polar bear–sized problems with two Double D batteries–sized preparation. We sometimes think major problems are going to be solved with the slightest of resources much to our demise.

Sooner or later, you will have an important meeting, athletic competition, sales presentation, class, test, or family event. You know you're not ready for it. You've been putting off the preparation because it is unpleasant or requires significant heavy lifting on your part. However, this level of preparation is the price needed for success. Failure to pay that price could have dire consequences.

The guides for Matt Dyer and his fellow hikers did not expect the polar bear to be so strong and determined. As a result, their level of expectation consisted of an electric fence powered by two Double D batteries. It almost cost Dyer his life. Likewise, if your level of preparation is at an unsatisfactory level, your level of expectation should be for an unsatisfactory result as well.

One of the defining characteristics of mighty leaders is courage. Hard conversations, difficult decisions, and moving forward in the face of uncertainty are constant companions. If you don't have courage, you simply cannot effectively lead.

In October 2022, a video of a mountain climber fending off an attacking black bear went viral. The harrowing scene taught leaders six things about the subject of courage.

First, courage is needed when you least expect it. As was previously mentioned, you are either in the middle of a storm, coming out of a storm, or heading into one. This particular climber probably never expected to encounter a black bear while climbing the face of a mountain. But as is so often the case, courage was required at a moment's notice.

Second, courage is a sign you are doing something that matters a great deal. Courage is not required in low-stakes environments. If a decision doesn't have much consequence, you do not need courage. The life of this climber was literally at stake. He could have been mauled by the bear or knocked off the side of the mountain, both probably resulting in certain death. Because the stakes were as high as it gets, life or death, courage was an absolute necessary.

Third, courage requires a full commitment from the one needing to show courage. Just like you cannot be half-pregnant, you cannot be half-courageous. This particular climber put all his physical, mental, and vocal energy into fighting off the bear. It took everything he had. And when courage is required from you, it will likely take everything you have as well.

Fourth, preparation activates courage. You do not know when a crisis will happen, but you can still prepare for one in advance. When encountering a bear in the wild, you are taught to utilize bear spray, scream loudly, and make a lot of noise. This climber was aware of those lessons and successfully used that training minus the spray. There are things in your industry which you know, if they happen, will cause a crisis. There are also things you don't know, like a pandemic, which cause a crisis as well. But as the leader, it is your responsibility to prepare yourself and your team to the best of your ability for those times. And when you do, courage will come a lot easier.

Fifth, courage is a continual necessity. When I first saw the video, I thought when the climber pushed the bear past him and it fell to the rock below, that would be the end of saga. But not so. The bear kept coming after him. We learned why at the twenty-three-second mark of the video. You can see the bear was protecting its baby cub. The lesson here for leaders is that issues are rarely resolved after an initial engagement. You must have the courage to address reoccurring issues over and over again.

Sixth, courage allows you to continue in your leadership. What I found most interesting about the video was when the bear finally ceased its attack and moved on, the climber resumed his climb up the mountain. His courage enabled him to continue his climb. Your courage will enable you to continue in your leadership climb as well.

DARREN HARRISON

One leader who is able to continue in his leadership because of his courage is Darren Harrison. Tuesday, May 10, 2022 started out as a normal afternoon for Harrison. He was flying from the Bahamas to Florida where he would see his pregnant wife, or so he thought. Suddenly, the pilot of their Cesna airplane had "gone incoherent." With the airplane now pilotless, Harrison got on the radio desperately looking for some form of assistance in landing the aircraft.

Air Traffic Controller Robert Morgan, who is also a certified flight instructor, immediately became engaged in the process. You may not face an issue as dire as an airplane crash, but the steps Morgan then took provide a template for any leader facing crisis situations.

It is important to remember crisis situations happen at inopportune times, once again at a moment's notice. Morgan said, "I rush over there and I walk in, and the room is really busy . . . and they're like, 'Hey, this pilot's incapacitated. The passengers are flying the plane. They have no flying experience.'" Notice the room was very busy. A lot was going on. The flight deck did not have the margin at the moment to handle a crisis situation of this magnitude. But challenging situations never come at opportune times. You must prepare in advance and then have the courage to press into the problem when it presents itself.

Seasoned leaders also know calmness provides clarity. Morgan said, "He was really calm. He said, 'I don't know how to fly. I don't know how to stop this thing if I do get on the runway.'" The challenge for all leaders is not to *act* calm during times of crisis but to actually *be* calm. By Harrison remaining calm, Morgan did not have to waste precious time and energy settling him down. He could immediately move toward solutions while instructing Harrison on safely landing the plane. Calmness provides clarity. It removes confusion. Remaining calm accelerates solutions and positive outcomes. So stay calm.

In addition to staying calm, leaders need to also give crisp, clear instructions during a crisis. When challenging times arise, simplicity is your friend. Leaders must utilize a brevity of language. Notice Morgan's instructions to Harrison. He said, "Try to hold the wings level and see if you can start descending for me. Push forward on the controls and descend at a very slow rate. Try to follow the coast either north- or southbound. We're trying to locate you." What is remarkable is only one word, "descending," was more than two syllables. Thirty words were one syllable; the other seven words were two syllables. This was by design and not a lack of vocabulary. During crisis situations, leaders should speak in a clear and concise manner.

Leaders should also prioritize reducing the margins of error. Smart coaches know the first step in learning how to win is to first learn how *not* to lose. Similarly, Morgan made the strategic decision to route the Cesna to the largest airport in the vicinity, Palm Beach International that was eight miles away. Morgan knew that the larger the airport, the higher the odds were for a desirable outcome. Morgan's objective was "he could just have a really big target to aim at." The larger airport provided longer runways for the plane to stop. During crisis situations, leaders can increase their team's odds of success by lowering their odds of failure. Give your team really big targets to aim at and really long runways to land on!

During times of crisis, things will not be ideal. They are going to be messy. The struggle will be real. You must strip away the non-essentials. Keep the main thing the main thing.

After the plane safely landed, Morgan said, "I felt like I was going to cry then because I had so much adrenaline built up. I was really happy that it worked out and that nobody got hurt." That was the objective—for the plane to land safely and nobody get hurt. Never confuse activity with accomplishment. With Morgan instructing Harrison every step of the way, the plane did safely land with no injuries or loss of life in the process. Mission accomplished.

When crisis situations have been successfully navigated, leaders should always give credit away. One of the reason leaders like Morgan exist is to guide and lead others when courage is required. It is during the most stressful situations when leaders are most needed. But when you successfully come out the other side, smart leaders should always give the credit to their teams. Referring to Harrison, Morgan said, "In my eyes, he was the hero. I was just doing my job."

In conclusion, crisis will eventually visit each and every one of us. The rain falls both on the just and the unjust. When those times come, remain calm, speak in clear and concise terms, remove margins of error, stay focused, and give credit to others afterward. By doing these things, you will better position yourself and your teams to successfully navigate crisis situations.

NICK BOSTIC

On July 11, just two months after Harrison's plane landing, Nick Bostic noticed a house on fire while driving in the city of Lafayette, Indiana. He immediately stopped his car and courageously ran into the burning home to help anyone inside who may be in danger.

He found an eighteen-year-old young woman babysitting her three younger siblings as well as a teenage friend of the family. The babysitter was able to get three of the children out, but after hearing a faint voice, Bostic then frantically searched the burning and smoke-filled home for the remaining child. He was able to locate the remaining child, a six-year-old girl name Kaylani on the second floor. While holding her in his arms, he broke out a second-floor window and jumped to the ground, saving Kaylani's life. He was then met by first responders who treated him for injuries and smoke inhalation. Bostic was released from the hospital two days later. We learn several lessons about courageous leadership from Nick Bostic:

First, people who courageously run into burning buildings while others are running out are heroes. It is in moments like this when we should all remember our first responders do things very similar to this every single day. Their commitment to serve and level of bravery is indescribable. The men and women who make up our armed forces, police, fire and rescue, EMTs, and medical personnel deserve our utmost respect, funding, and support.

Second, courage requires action, not just words. Bostic could have easily called 9-1-1 as he headed toward his destination and reported a house fire. Others may have stopped and simply watched from a safe distance. However, there was something innately grafted into Bostic's character that when he came upon a burning house and the potential danger faced by those inside, his involvement required more than just a phone call or being a concerned bystander. He needed to personally get involved at a deeper level, a level which he knew would have a personal cost. Bostic needed to take a risk and immediately engage the issue.

He told WLFI-TV, "I slammed on the brakes, I turned the steering wheel, I did a 180. I ran into the back of the house and I was yelling for anybody. Four faces, three or four faces, came out the top."

Third, we also learn courageous people are more concerned about the safety of others than their own. When Bostic and Kaylani made it safely to the street, his first response was not about his injured arm or difficulty breathing due to smoke inhalation. Police body cameras showed the first thing he asked was, "Is the baby OK? Please tell me the baby's OK." He was more concerned about the baby than himself.

Fourth, courage comes with a significant cost. People love the perks of leadership, but so few are willing to pay the price. Bostic paid a significant physical price to help rescue those in the house. But as he also told WLFI-TV, "It was all worth it. I kept reminding myself what a small sacrifice. This temporary pain . . . it's so worth it." David Barrett, the four siblings' father, would agree. He told *The Washington Post*, "He's a real hero, and my daughter's a real hero for waking the kids up. I don't like to think about what might have happened if Nick hadn't shown up. I'm grateful beyond words." As was also heard in the bodycam footage, a police officer on the scene said, "You did good, dude." Yes, he did. Bostic did really, really good.

Fifth, we learn that a generous act of courage is often met by an equal or greater generous response. Bostic cared enough to give up his time and personal agenda to stop and help a family in desperate need. He then risked his life by running into a burning home. Bostic physically injured himself, breaking out a window with his arm. He then jumped from the same second-floor window. Bostic inhaled unhealthy levels of smoke, suffered first-degree burns, and spent time in the hospital. These are extraordinary examples of courage, bravery, and generosity.

Unfortunately, Bostic's stay in the hospital would result in sizable medical expenses. However, no need to worry. Ralph Waldo Emerson once said, "It is one of the true compensations of this life that a man cannot help another, without also helping himself." As of July 20, 2022, a Go Fund Me page set up to cover his medical expenses had already raised more than $470,000. Bostic would also be honored by the city.

Ike Reighard, senior pastor of Piedmont Church in Marietta, Georgia, once taught me the safest place to be in a fire is where it has already burned. I'm sure Nick Bostic would agree.

PASTOR TODD KORASICK

Air traffic controllers and first responders obviously need courage to be successful in their jobs. Another industry which requires incredible courage is pastoring a local church. Let me start my explanation by asking a pointed question. Pastors and church leaders, what is your excuse for not being obedient to move forward with the vision God has given you and your church? It is often said that church leaders do not need two reasons to say "No" to something. They only need one reason to pause and put anything on hold.

Todd Korasick, the lead pastor of Monett Community Church in Monett, Missouri, had significant reasons to not move forward with the church's expansion and capital campaign. First, there was the reality of COVID. But in 2019, he was also diagnosed with Stage 3 melanoma cancer. But he and the church had the faith and courage to move forward anyway. But the question was why, especially when it would be so easy to delay? After all, many pastors pause their ministry initiatives for far less compelling reasons than COVID and cancer.

Monettt, Missouri, is a rural community located in the southwest portion of the state. It is populated by only 9,000 people but swells to 25,000 during the week because of industry. Pastor Todd told me that like most cities regardless of size, fewer than 15 percent of those within a twenty-mile radius attend a local church. When he arrived in 2018, he felt a deep calling to make an eternal impact in rural America for Jesus. And he and the church began doing so.

The church grew from 125 in weekly attendance to over 300 in less than two years! But more people needed to be reached, and the church was out of worship and children's space. It was time to expand and raise capital. Working with INJOY Stewardship, the church embarked on a capital campaign—and then COVID hit—and the cancer continued. But the calling God had placed on Pastor Todd's heart still remained.

Once the church reopened, Pastor Todd and the church leadership were faced with yet another issue. Attendance was down, but God had still given them a vision. Pastor Todd told me, "We don't have the packed-out building (because of 2020's pandemic), but we do have the vision of what could be." They remained obedient to funding and facilitating the vision which God had given them because it had not changed.

Now cancer-free, Pastor Todd was still receiving treatments and infusion therapies while leading the church through its campaign. When I asked where his passion and energy to lead came from, he responded, "The vision is bigger than me. I saw God leading in such a way, and we saw God continuing to bless and God continuing to change lives and continue to bring people through our doors that desperately needed Jesus. And, I just saw that and the energy behind the vision of what we were trying to accomplish was what continued to drive me."

Led by Pastor Todd's inspiration and faithfulness to what God had called the church to do, the results of the campaign were simply astonishing! The campaign far exceeded expectations, and lives are once-again being changed on a weekly basis. At the time is this writing, children's attendance has now returned to pre-COVID numbers.

Pastor Todd concluded our conversation by acknowledging that every time you face change, there will be fear. But you must have the courage to press forward regardless because the mission is too important not to. He said, "We want to be a church that's reaching the unchurched in rural America, and there's tens of thousands of people around me who desperately need Him." And might I add, they desperately need Monnett Community Church as well.

HARD CONVERSATIONS

Leadership requires the courage to have hard conversations. Not to be hyperbolic or dramatic, but hard conversations could potentially prevent tragedy and save a life. Let me give you a sobering example.

As a society, we have been cheated by having Nick Saban as just a football coach. Sure, he has provided countless hours of athletic entertainment and the impact on the young men he has coached during his career cannot be quantified. However, can you imagine if Nick Saban were a scientist or United States president? Our country and world could potentially look like the University of Alabama's football program.

Coach Saban was speaking to the Alabama Football Coaches Association and addressed the topic of Henry Ruggs's tragic car accident in the early hours of November 2, 2021. This devastating event resulted in the loss of his athletic career, being incarcerated for the majority if not the rest of his adult life, and most importantly, the death of an innocent young woman.

During his speech, Coach Saban said, "People are more apprehensive about being leaders than they've ever been before because they're worried about what everybody thinks." I agree. Leadership is often a lonely place. Unpopular decisions and hard conversations come with the territory, and leaders must have the courage to be willing to stand alone amidst harsh criticism. Conviction and mental toughness are required. This is a price more and more leaders are now unwilling to pay.

Coach Saban then brought a sobering message. Referring to Ruggs, he said:

> If there was a player in Las Vegas who was drinking at 3 o'clock in the morning with his buddies and his girlfriend and somebody would have taken his keys away, probably would have pissed him off, probably would have made him mad, probably wouldn't have thought very much of you for doing that. But would he be better off now or is he better off where he was going 156 miles per hour and running his #@& into somebody and killing them? And he's in jail and doesn't have a career anymore.

Saban asked the following questions of those closest to Ruggs, "So what kind of friend were you? What kind of leader were you when you allowed the guy to do it? But nobody wants to do that because they're afraid of what somebody's going to think of them."

So what makes someone a good friend? Sometimes it is not what you think. Being a good friend is having the courage to do what is best for that person regardless of the circumstance and whether they appreciate it or not at the current moment. To say Ruggs did not have good friends with him that night would be a tragic understatement. As leaders we must all ask, are we more concerned about what someone thinks of us or what is in that person's best interest?

SEATTLE SEAHAWKS

"We need to have a hard conversation." No one wants to hear those seven words. If you hear this statement, it often means things have gone terribly wrong in your church, family, business, or athletic organization. It indicates things have declined to a very unhealthy level and changes are desperately needed.

On February 1, 2015, one of the most famous plays in NFL history took place. The Seattle Seahawks were trailing the New England Patriots by the score of 28–24 in Super Bowl XLIX. The Seahawks had the ball on the Patriots 1-yard line with twenty-seven seconds remaining in the game. Conventional wisdom was to have quarterback Russell Wilson hand the ball to the team's star running back, Marshawn Lynch, for what surely would be the game-winning touchdown.

However, head coach Pete Carroll called for a pass play. As discussed in Annie Duke's excellent book *Thinking in Bets: Making Smarter Decisions When You Don't Have All the Facts,* this was statistically not a bad decision. In addition, the process for making it was quite sound. However, the result was horrifying. The Patriots' Malcolm Butler intercepted Wilson's pass at the goal line preserving the team's victory.

Immediately afterward, the team became emotionally, psychologically, and relationally fractured. Fingers were being pointed. Blame was being assigned. Trust in team leadership was in danger of becoming permanently lost. For the team to move forward the following season, hard conversations needed to happen so healing could begin. Wilson stepped up to facilitate the process.

He organized a working vacation for eighty-five teammates and family members in Hawaii. Sensing the high tension and poor morale, the trip was designed for everyone to air their differences and attempt to rebuild team unity. In the September 7, 2015, edition of *Sports Illustrated,* author Greg Bishop chronicled the team's trip. As I read his account, I gleaned several keys to successfully having hard conversations.

First, you must admit hard conversations are needed. A leader's primary responsibility is to properly evaluate reality. Wilson intuitively knew the Seahawks needed to iron out their differences. Therefore, he initiated and then facilitated the hard conversations. In Hawaii, all the team's leaders were present except Earl Thomas who was rehabbing an injury. The meeting's primary leaders were Wilson and key locker room voices wide receiver Doug Baldwin and safety Kam Chancellor. Baldwin said, "Kam was pivotal. He's like the godfather of the locker room. Any problems, any issues, you go to him."

Second, hard conversations require the courage to have brutal honesty. Unfiltered information is a necessity. Nothing was off limits about the team, the coaches, its personnel, how decisions were made, and why the Seahawks lost the Super Bowl. Hard conversations are often harsh but necessary if you want to create an environment where everyone can get their issues into the open and move forward.

As a result, hard conversations are usually filled with tension. Healthy teams wrestle with tension and understand tension is necessary for growth. They don't run from tension; they run to tension. For hard conversations to be their most effective, they require everyone's participation. Passivity, disengagement, and lack of transparency are the enemies of a hard conversations. They are not one-way discussions. The team's first meeting took over forty-five minutes, with everyone sharing their initial thoughts.

Their time together increased accountability. Hard questions were asked. People were forced to take responsibility for their actions and role in the team's success and failure. Issues were brought into the open. Baldwin said, "There were a lot of questions that needed to be answered. And a lot that needed to be asked."

Wilson put a lot of effort into making this time together as productive as possible. First, he had meticulously scheduled every moment of the trip. This included morning workouts, afternoon trips, and team dinners. Their conversations were also based upon a foundation of success. Every evening the team watched motivational videos which included team highlights from their biggest wins.

If done right, hard conversations improve performance, solve problems, regain lost momentum, (re)build team chemistry, and ensure future success. Baldwin said, "We were forced to be vulnerable. And that made us closer . . . We didn't know if the trip was going to work. We still don't." Ironically, those hard, dare I say, courageous conversations ultimately did not work. The result of Coach Carroll's much-debated decision to have Wilson throw a pass rather than hand the ball to Lynch fractured the team's locker room. What should have been a football dynasty was never the same again.

I hope your hard conversations have more success than the Seattle Seahawks, but they still needed to take place regardless of the outcome. Everyone on the team would have regretted the potential missed opportunities of what could have been had they chose to remain silent.

During hard conversations if unhealthy conflict breaks out, motivational speaker, entrepreneur, and leadership expert Tony Robbins offers the following five tips for diffusing arguments.

1. Recognize your patterns. This includes destructive behaviors like reliving the past, avoiding confrontation which leads to bigger arguments, competing to be heard, and not being present.

2. Stop accusing the other person.

3. Use the right tone. Thirty-eight percent of your vocal elements are communicated in ways other than words.

4. Listen. Forty-five percent of your time communicating is used for listening. To be a better listener avoid distractions, use body language, summarize the conversation, and ask great questions.

5. Defuse the argument. Take a breath. Say, "Let's start over." Use humor. If these do not work, show compassion.

ANIMAL RAIN

Yes, you read the previous words correctly. On Wednesday, December 30, 2021, fish were literally raining from the Texarkana, Texas, sky. These small animals appear to have been sucked up into a waterspout and fell back to earth when the spout subsided. Believe it or not, though unusual, this event known as "animal rain" is not uncommon.

When a waterspout has enough power to generate what is called an updraft and the fish are the right size and located in the right spot, the spout's vortex can lift them up before eventually dropping them back toward the earth.

This story was so fascinating I had to extract the leadership lessons from it. The following are three tips for handling unexpected leadership problems I think we can learn from this ecological anomaly:

First, most issues we face are not uncommon. When something *bizarre* or *crazy* happens in our life and leadership, it can shake our foundation. Courage will be required. But the fact is we rarely face problems unique only to us. Others have often faced similar obstacles and actually have overcome them. For instance, did you know Oroville, California, had a raining fish problem in 2017? Also, the Weather Channel reported that the Australian town of Lajamanu has had multiple cases of animal rain. The problem is to always identify the real problem; the solution, then, becomes obvious because it has been faced many times before.

Second, great chaos creates great opportunity. Smart leaders always see chaos as an opportunity. For instance, the most successful investors see downturns in the economy as yard sales for the rich. Similarly, many town residents saw the animal rain as an opportunity. One man used the small fish as fishing bait. Others simply had a large fish fry. They made the best use out this unusual circumstance.

Finally, we learn the value of discretion. While this is an interesting story, it did not end well for the fish. They had a fatal return to earth. Smart leaders use discretion and know which storms not to get sucked up in to. Pick your battles and storms carefully. The wrong ones can be fatal to your leadership. Sometimes you need to avoid the vortex. Oftentimes, it is best to remain silent or just walk away. Otherwise, the storm may spit you out as well, and you will come crashing back to earth.

In conclusion, it was raining fish in Texarkana, and they made something positive out of it. If you experience something unusual in your leadership, use the three lessons listed above to make the best of your situation as well.

JORDAN SPIETH

Someone whose discretion was in question was three-time PGA major championship winner Jordan Spieth. On Saturday, February 5, 2022, Spieth hit an errant shot on the eighth hole of the AT&T Pebble Beach Pro-Am Tournament. The ball landed just inches from dropping off a seventy-foot cliff. Rather than taking a drop and replaying the ball, Spieth literally risked his life by standing on the cliff's edge to hit a miraculous shot to save par.

As leaders, we can sometimes find ourselves standing on our own leadership cliff. When these times arise, Spieth's shot teaches us several lessons about how we should handle ourselves when facing perilous situations.

First, we often face going off a leadership cliff because of our own previous bad decisions. Oftentimes, we have to own the role we played in being on the leadership cliff and take accountability for it. As previously mentioned, Spieth was forced into this situation because of an errant shot. How many errant leadership shots have we hit, which put us in uncertain situations?

Second, as we discussed in the first chapter with Dak Prescott, we must practice crisis situations to avoid going off a leadership cliff. Leaders will either prepare or repair. One of the trademarks of Spieth's game is his ability to make difficult and awkward shots. He has obviously spent countless hours practicing those situational conditions. As previously mentioned, the more you practice crisis situations, the better prepared you will be when they present themselves, and that will activate courage.

Third, to avoid going off a leadership cliff, get your bearings down. Spieth could have taken a drop to move his ball. No one would have blamed him. But instead, he remained calm and made sure he had solid footing.

That leads to the final point. To avoid going off a leadership cliff, execute the fundamentals. Courage and doing the basics go hand-in-hand. Because he had gotten his bearings down, Spieth was then able to strike the ball effectively and set himself up for a ten-foot putt for par.

When facing a leadership cliff, the following are best practices:

1. Stay calm;
2. Make sure the fundamentals of your organization are solid;
3. Stabilize your footing; and
4. Execute.

Leadership cliffs are scary for even the most experienced leaders. Spieth told a CBS reporter at the close of the round, "I'm glad I finished the round and didn't fall off that cliff on eight." He added, "It was by far the most nerve-wracking shot I've ever hit.... It was awfully close. I've never had a life and death situation on a shot before. So I thought I wouldn't really have nerves the rest of the day after that one."

As leaders, we are all faced from time-to-time with situations, which bring us to our knees. It is during those times our metal is tested. Perhaps you're going through such a situation right now. Hopefully, it is not a life-and-death situation like the one faced by Spieth.

BIG E'S BROKEN NECK

One athlete who faced potentially tragic circumstances with immeasurable courage, gratefulness, and positivity is Ettore Ewen. You may know him better as World Wrestling Entertainment (WWE) superstar Big E. On the March 11, 2022, live edition of WWE's *Smackdown* originating from Birmingham, Alabama, Big E suffered a broken neck after landing on his head outside of ring.

Everyone watching in person or on television immediately knew Big E was hurt, and something was wrong. Television cameras locked in on the in-ring action for the remainder of Big E's tag team match while emergency personnel assisted the wrestler on the floor. During a commercial break, fans watched the wrestler being wheeled out on a stretcher. People were slightly relieved as Big E gave the "thumbs up" signal to the crowd, indicating he was fine.

But shortly thereafter, Big E released a video from the hospital to give fans an unfortunate update on his condition. Though he had movement "in all his digits," Big E had suffered a broken neck. Because of the positive attitude he displayed, Big E provided a wonderful example on how to courageously handle significant adversity.

Big E is a world-class athlete and obviously in superior shape. But pain, tragedy, misfortune, and difficult times do not discriminate. Sooner or later, they unexpectedly visit all of us, no matter how smart, talented, rich, or strong we may be. Big E reminds us to be grateful for every moment we have because life is paper-tissue thin and can change in an instant.

Leaders should also properly evaluate reality during difficult times. Though Big E was hopeful, he was also realistic. While moving his fingers, he said, "I can move all my digits. You see that? That's nice. That's always a good thing. Strength feels fine, but unfortunately right now, they tell me my neck is broken. So there's that." During difficult times we must all reach a point where we face reality and say, "So there's that."

As has been stated many times, leaders always point to a brighter tomorrow. Leaders must be dealers of hope, especially during difficult times. Big E said, "I'll be all right. I'll be good. Don't worry. Go to sleep. Don't worry about 'ole me."

The fact that Big E would be concerned about others and comforting them while he was in such pain and uncertainty is extraordinary. Watching the video reminds us the quickest way to lessen our problems is to place our focus on other people. It doesn't make our issues disappear, but it does make them easier to manage.

Big E's gimmick is one of positivity which clearly is an extension of his real-life personality. His focus on others and having a positive attitude after learning of a broken neck was remarkable. May we all handle our difficult times with half as much selflessness, positivity, and optimism as he did. This is how courageous leaders like Benaiah and Big E behave.

Having this level of courage will help you become mighty and move people from pandemic to progress.

CHAPTER 6 STUDY AND DISCUSSION QUESTIONS

Benaiah showed great courage by confronting and overcoming significant opposition. What significant challenges have you recently faced which required great courage from you?

_____

_____

_____

What did you learn from Ukrainian President Volodymyr Zelensky about the subject of courage?

_____

_____

_____

When an unexpected crisis hits your family or organization, does your courage inspire others to continue moving forward? What evidence would you give for your answer?

_____

_____

_____

Are there any hard conversations you need to have which you have put off? If so, what is preventing you from taking action?

_____

_____

_____

Are you currently facing any leadership cliffs? If so, what fundamentals are you relying on to successfully navigate the situation?

_____

_____

_____

CHAPTER 7

Faith

"And the Lord brought about a great victory that day."
—2 Samuel 23:10 (ESV)

"and the Lord worked a great victory."
—2 Samuel 23:12 (ESV)

As we close out this book, teaching you how to become mighty and move from pandemic to progress, we finish with the most important skill of all—faith.

You may be producing record results at your organization. In regard to passion, you may own the results of your team at a level no one else does. You may have the resilience of a national championship quarterback or tsunami survivor. It may be obvious you are an incredible team builder. You seem to intuitively recognize people's strengths and know how to best leverage their unique giftedness. It just comes naturally for you.

In terms of self-leadership, inner peace and contentment marks your life. You not only know your team's strengths and areas for growth, your self-awareness allows you to know yours as well. Finally, you may have the courage of a national leader fending off an invasion or a camper fighting off a bear.

You may be doing all of these things, but what the two scriptures listed above remind us of is that unless the Lord brings the victory, all our efforts will be in vain. Our efforts will end in futility. Yes, we may have some short-term success, but to become mighty and move from pandemic to progress, it will only come with the Lord's supernatural intervention.

PREMARITAL QUESTIONS

Where I needed supernatural intervention in 2022 was with my daughter Anna meeting her future husband Jonathan and eventually getting married. When Jonathan asked me for permission to marry Anna, I walked him through a series of questions I felt were necessary to having a successful marriage.

Most couples think engagement is about preparing for a wedding. While this two-to-four-hour event certainly seems all-consuming, I am much more interested in what happens the following twenty-to-forty years. I told Jonathan to let Anna and her mother Sonya work out all the wedding details as he needs to focus on planning a life. The precedent for this advice is Adam and Eve. Adam already had a home in the Garden and a job tending to it. He had a life, and then God brought Eve into the equation to help him. Jonathan needed to have his life in order before bringing Anna into it.

I have found much of the pre-marital counseling couples receive is woefully lacking in preparing them for the real-life issues that can sink a marriage. As a result and because I want to see them have a thriving relationship, I asked Jonathan a different level of questions.

The following are eighteen questions I asked, and engaged couples should answer, prior to getting married:

1. Set the tone early. If one of you is sexually unsatisfied, how are you going to handle it? Are you going to talk about it together or handle it internally? If you handle it internally, are you going to suppress your feelings and if so, for how long? Or are you going to seek out more destructive solutions?

2. Let's talk about finances, the number one cause of divorce. What are you willing to go in debt over?

3. Who will handle the budget?

4. How will each person handle it when the budget says, "No, you can't buy that" or "Not yet; we have to wait"?

5. Regarding conflict, how do you argue? What are the lines you don't cross?

6. Do both of you say, "I'm sorry," or is it one person who always yields and/or takes the blame? Because if both don't say "I'm sorry" on a regular basis, the other will resent it sooner or later.

7. Where are you going to spend holidays and why?

8. How many children are you going to have?

9. How are you going to discipline these children?

10. What type of education will they have—homeschool, private, or public and why?

11. What are you willing to miss church over?

12. What do the two of you think of tithing?

13. After a hard day at work, you both come home tired and exhausted. Who handles dinner?

14. What are you willing to watch or not watch on television? Where's the line on sexual content and language?

15. Is it acceptable to have deep friendships with the opposite sex? Will you ever travel, have a meal, or be behind closed doors with the opposite sex?

16. What type of birth control are you going to use, who is going to use it, and why?

17. How will you handle it if one of your children wants to transition?

18. Is there ever a reason for divorce in your mind?

These are the real-life issues every couple must deal with. They don't have to be caught off guard or say, "I wish I knew this before getting married." If they are on the same page with these questions heading into the wedding, they have a chance at having a long-lasting, God-honoring marriage.

MOVIE NIGHT

As the wedding drew closer, I was ambushed one evening by emotion and sentimentality. Anna and I were on the sofa, watching two of our favorite movies, *The Princess Diaries* and *The Princess Diaries 2: Royal Engagement*. At the conclusion of the second film, I looked over at her and said, "We're not going to have very many more of these Saturday night movies on the sofa." She responded by saying, "Oh, you're going to make me emotional," to which I replied, "Don't get emotional. You're going to have a new guy for your Saturday nights very soon."

When I watched her walk up the stairs to go to bed for the evening, I realize not only will there not be very more Saturday night movies, but also not many more nights of her heading up the stairs.

It was then I felt a great sense of pride—and a great sense of sadness.

THE FATHER OF THE BRIDE

The time eventually arrived when I walked Anna down the aisle to marry the man of her dreams. Giving my life to Christ and marrying my wife Sonya are the two most important days of my life. Everything good which has happened in my life flowed from those two moments. But giving my daughter's hand in marriage and the following reception was the most fun day of my life.

In reflection, I want to give you seven life-changing leadership lessons I experienced from being The Father of the Bride. Enjoy!

The Night Before the Wedding

The night before the wedding I could not sleep. It wasn't because of the hotel's flat pillows, hard mattress, or the inability to regulate the room temperature. No, it was because I was wide awake and filled with regret. What kept going through my mind were all the mistakes I ever made as a father and how I wished I would have done a better job.

I completely disagree with people who say, "I wouldn't change anything about my past because that's what made me the person I am today." First, you might be a better person today if you did not make those mistakes in the past. Second, other's lives might be better if you did not make those mistakes. Third, I would love to have a number of do-overs. I thought of many times I wasn't sensitive enough or how I should have given her more of my time. Knowing girls often marry someone just like their father, I hoped I had set a good example.

I know I got some sleep because of stress dreams but I don't know how much. Ultimately, I woke up with an overwhelming sense of guilt and sadness. All I could think of was, where did the time go and why did I waste so much of it?

But shortly after 7:00 a.m., I received a text from Anna. She was asking my advice on how to handle a certain situation she was facing that day. To her, it was just a question, but to me this was much, much more. It was both a comforting and confirming gift from God. It was as if He was telling me how much my daughter loved me and still wanted my advice. I wasn't perfect, but I wasn't all bad either.

The Leadership Lesson—"Children are a gift from the LORD; they are a reward from him" (Ps. 127:3, NLT). Enjoy every moment you can with your children because time flies by. That is what moments are, just moments. As we previously noted, they last for a moment, and then they are gone. Also, this is a reminder to live the type of life where you will have no regrets.

The First Viewing

The image I have always had in mind of Anna was her in a onesie sitting on my lap as I read books to her. She seemed to hang on every word I said. Those type of memories become entrenched in your mind forever. Well, a couple of hours before the wedding, I was escorted to an offsite location for pictures and my initial viewing of Anna in another onesie, but this onesie just happened to be long and white. It was her wedding dress. My little girl had turned into such a beautiful young woman, it took my breath away and brought tears to my eyes.

The Leadership Lesson—Properly evaluate reality. My daughter was no longer a toddler. In fact, she was a beautiful young lady. The reality is she had been one for quite some time.

The Letter to the Father

It was then she presented both Sonya and I letters written for the occasion. I was unaware it is now customary for the bride to write letters to each of her parents in conjunction with the initial viewing. If this is an Instagram tradition, I'll take it. I will cherish the words Anna wrote for the rest of my life. I have had the privilege of accumulating many special items in my life. But nothing, and I mean *nothing*, will ever mean as much to me as the letter Anna wrote.

The Leadership Lesson—It is incomprehensible and impossible to describe how much a father loves his daughter.

The Calm Before the Vows

As I picked Anna up to drive her to the wedding venue, she was understandably nervous and anxious. Anna wanted to stay in motion as much as possible. Movement kept her mind active and not focused on the enormity of the moment. So we literally drove around the parking lot for about five minutes. I was concerned about giving the lady in the backseat motion sickness, but hey, whatever the bride wants, the bride gets!

Once the families had been escorted down the aisle to their seats, it was just Anna, me, and two ladies holding the train of her dress left in the back. She couldn't move but wanted to stay in motion. So I said, "Hey, dance with me." She and I then proceeded to dance in place bringing one of the ladies holding her train to tears.

We then began our walk down the aisle. I asked her how slow she wanted to walk. She said, "I want to go fast," and away we went. Anna indicated her veil felt like it might be falling off her head, so I told her I would keep an eye on it. Because of our fast pace and my focus on her veil, the next thing I knew we were standing in front of the pastor and groom.

This moment was a picture of the last twenty-three years. Anna was moving fast, and I was watching her back. And we got to where we were going way too quickly.

The Leadership Lesson—A friend advised me to walk slowly during every moment of the weekend and enjoy creating the memories I would never forget. This advice was spot-on. During life-changing moments, walk slowly and take it all in.

The Reception

Anna is a program director at the church where she works. Because she enjoys the creative process, Anna programmed a masterpiece of a reception. Two words made it especially fun—glow sticks! Everyone was given glow sticks for the reception. Let me just say, almost anyone can become a good dancer when waving glow sticks.

The Leadership Lesson—Let people play to their strengths. Everyone wins when this happens.

The Morning After

"But Mary kept all these things, and pondered them in her heart" (Luke 2:19, KJV). These words were written after Mary had just given birth to her new baby boy, Jesus.

I took a walk on the beach the morning after the wedding. It was a bright sunny morning, about seventy degrees and not a cloud in the sky. The sea was calm, providing the quiet crash of small waves slowly rolling in, and there was no one else within hundreds of yards. I was walking slowly, with water slightly below my knees. Everything was perfect. Similar to Mary, I simply pondered all of the weekend's events and the last twenty-three years with Anna in my heart. It was a holy moment of reflection, gratefulness, joy, and worship.

The Leadership Lesson—The greatest leader ever is Jesus Christ and He is our generous God. "Every good gift and every perfect gift is from above, coming down from the Father of lights, with whom there is no variation or shadow due to change" (James 1:17, ESV). Raising Anna and watching her grow up was a good and perfect gift.

The Money

Let's now get pragmatic and address the elephant in the room. At the end of the day, the money doesn't matter. Were we over our budget? Of course. Was it worth it? Every single day of the week and twice on Sunday.

Let the budget be a guideline, but in reality, there really is not a budget. If you do have a budget, I would say add 10 percent to it. Sorry, Dave Ramsey! Hopefully, this event will only happen once, and the joy of it will eclipse any cost that was paid. After all, can you truly put a cost on the memories made? I can't.

The Leadership Lesson—Smart leaders know the difference between value and cost and choose value every single time.

HIGHLY EFFECTIVE FATHERS

I love being a father. The purpose of the family is for procreation and the proclamation of the Gospel by passing it from one generation to the next. With this in mind, the following are what I have found to be twenty-five practices of highly effective fathers:

1. Highly effective fathers love Jesus. You cannot be the most effective earthly father possible if you do not have a healthy relationship with your heavenly Father.

2. Highly effective fathers love the Scriptures. Godly fathers instill in their child's lives a love of the Scriptures and elevate the Scriptures to a point of primacy.

3. Highly effective fathers have fun with their children. Children truly are a treasure from the Lord. Enjoying your children and having fun is a choice. Being a parent can be tough, but I choose to enjoy the times I have with my daughter.

4. Highly effective fathers are not passive. They actively engage their children's lives. Men have been fighting passivity since the Garden. Effective fathers are always present.

5. Highly effective fathers protect their families. They would literally die for them.

6. Highly effective fathers sense and seize opportunities with their children. As a parent, the days are long, but the seasons are short. We are not promised tomorrow and must take advantage of every possible moment to connect with our children.

7. Highly effective fathers make wise decisions. When we are on our death beds and preparing to take our last breaths, our thoughts will

not be on work-related items. Each day we have a choice. Are we going to love that person in front of us or not?

8. Highly effective fathers are highly motivated. Being a parent can be tiring. We must often summon up every last bit of energy we have to be fully present.

9. Highly effective fathers leave a godly legacy. There are many competing voices in a father's life. It is the equity in the relationships you build up with your children over the years that is the most important thing in parenting.

10. Highly effective fathers celebrate milestones. Birthdays, anniversaries, family vacations, holidays, and yes, weddings are a *big* deal. Highly effective fathers celebrate these days and make them memorable.

11. Highly effective fathers deeply love their children's mother. There is a good chance that all men, if we're lucky enough to live long enough, are going to need our wives to help us get dressed one day. There are few pictures in this world more beautiful than this type of lifelong sacrificial love.

12. Highly effective fathers model the type of man their daughters will one day marry. Men, do you want your daughter to marry someone just like you? The reality is she most likely will. I speak from experience.

13. Highly effective fathers sing and dance with their daughters. It makes her feel like Cinderella.

14. Highly effective fathers are noticed by the world. In a time when selfish and dysfunctional behavior are the norm, emotionally

healthy fathers who put Christ and their families first are noticed by everyone in their sphere of influence.

15. Highly effective fathers are generous. Parenting is expensive. Medical bills, schooling, weddings, shoes and apparel, sports, and other items come with a high price. Anything valuable costs money. Highly effective fathers are willing to pay whatever price is necessary to bless their children.

16. Highly effective fathers honor their parents. They model how to love the different generations within the family

17. Highly effective fathers do not discourage their children.

18. Highly effective fathers do not provoke their children to anger. They aren't jerks to their children.

19. Highly effective fathers are effective providers. They do what is necessary to put food on the table.

20. Highly effective fathers bring stability to their homes. Great fathers are men of peace and love.

21. Highly effective fathers are disciplinarians.

22. But highly effective fathers are also compassionate.

23. Highly effective fathers are effective teachers. You can be a teacher and not a great leader. But you cannot be a great leader without being a great teacher. You must show your children not only where to go but also equip them on how to get there.

24. Highly effective fathers create generational wealth.

25. Highly effective fathers love their children unconditionally. For many fathers, everyone wants something from them. Their relationships are transactional. They are conditional and based solely on performance. For fathers, there is great comfort and safety, which can only be found in a loving home.

Fathers, how did you measure up to this list twenty-five practices? What areas can you improve on starting today?

GROWING CHURCHES DURING THE PANDEMIC

Moving from being a father to becoming the father of the bride was not possible without the Lord giving me the victory. But just as my individual family grew in 2022, the Lord gave victory to many church families across America and grew them as well during the pandemic. In fact, 17,000 local congregations (or 5 percent of all US churches) actually grew in onsite attendance during the pandemic of 2020 and early 2021.

In February 2022, I had the privilege of attending the Defy The Odds Conference hosted by Rock Springs Church in Milner, Georgia, and its senior pastor Benny Tate. During the event's closing session, Pastor Benny discussed six common threads these 17,000 churches had which led to increased onsite weekend attendance during the pandemic.

First was external prayer. While these churches obviously prayed for people inside the church, they also aggressively focused their prayers outwardly. They placed an emphasis on praying for people who did not go to church prior to the pandemic. They did what is called Pray-And-Go. These churches would drive to houses in targeted communities and pray over whomever lived there. They would pray for their mental and physical health as well as their spiritual condition. Prior to leaving, they would leave a doorhanger, letting them know they were not alone and were being prayed for.

Second, they celebrated more. God never left His throne in 2020 and 2021. He was still in the transformation business the entire time. Growing churches constantly celebrated what God *was* doing in the lives of people. They were not just focused on all the challenges. This kept people focused on the mission and vision, kept morale high, and generated much-needed momentum for their staff and key leaders.

Third, they expanded their online presence. Churches who were evangelistic and outwardly focused made an interesting discovery. They learned a growing online audience did not take away from their live attendance. By leveraging digital services as a front door, it actually drove more and more people into the building. Digital is an embarrassingly poor substitute for live attendance, but done right, it will increase the number of those physically present.

Fourth was a monthly evangelistic emphasis. Many churches conducted an annual Friend Day or some other big event for which the people could invite their unchurched friends to prior to the pandemic. The churches that grew in onsite attendance during the pandemic actually turned up their evangelistic efforts by doing monthly major events rather than just an annual one.

Fifth, they fostered churches. The churches who grew in live attendance focused on the big-C Church, not just their own local church. Churches who were generous to other churches in the community in terms of money and volunteers saw their own churches grow. You cannot put anything into a closed fist, only an open hand. This basic principle applies to churches who grew as well.

Finally, churches who grew during the pandemic decided there would be no more excuses. Failure to grow was not an option. It was time to quit using COVID (or Delta or Omicron or the flu or inflation or whatever is next) as an excuse for a lack of growth.

Churches with a combined focus on external prayer, celebration, leveraging their online presence, conducting monthly evangelistic efforts, investing in partner churches, and stopped making excuses saw attendance increases during the pandemic.

GROWING CHURCHES POST-PANDEMIC

I have a unique job with INJOY Stewardship Solutions in that I only work with growing churches. My day consists of interacting with some of God's finest leaders and choicest servants. These individuals need more money to build new facilities or retire debt so they can do more ministry. The position I hold affords me the privilege of having a front-row seat to current best practices in church growth. Allow me to give you some thoughts on what growing churches are doing post-pandemic.

The Bible records the following words written to the church of Ephesus in Revelation 2:2–5

> I know your works, your toil and your patient endurance, and how you cannot bear with those who are evil, but have tested those who call themselves apostles and are not, and found them to be false. I know you are enduring patiently and bearing up for my name's sake, and you have not grown weary. But I have this against you, that you have abandoned the love you had at first. Remember therefore from where you have fallen; repent, and do the works you did at first. If not, I will come to you and remove your lampstand from its place, unless you repent. (ESV)

Can I paraphrase for modern attractional church audiences?

> I know you put on great services. I know you have hazers (smoke machines). I know you have incredible lights. I know you look like Disney. I know you work hard in the community. I know you speak out against social injustice. I know your sermons are relevant, and you have wonderful illustrations and transitions. I know you produce things with excellence. I know you're trendy. I know your staff and volunteers are skilled. I just have one thing against you—You have forgotten your first love—Me!

Churches who are growing post-pandemic are led by leaders who are marked by personal holiness. They have spent intimate time with the Lord. These leaders are deeply rooted in the Scriptures and place a high priority on doing what God says. They exude the fruit of the Spirit. Prayer, brokenness, and dependence on the Holy Spirit's redemptive work in their lives are their brand.

Does the Attractional Church model still work? No—and Yes.

No. Lights, sound, the cool-factor and the weekend presentation still need to be done with excellence. But COVID stripped away all non-essentials. People are scared. They know their world can be upended instantly. Many lost careers, influence, income, opportunities, hope, and even loved ones. Their children are struggling with identity issues. Geopolitical and environmental concerns are constants. Their lives are unstable and the future is uncertain. Hazers, strobe lights, and rhymes no longer fill the void they currently have. People need real answers, which can only be found in the person of Jesus Christ.

But Yes, attractional churches still work. The attractional church still works if you know what people are attracted to. People are now attracted to leaders who teach the Bible and tell them what God says about the issues of their lives. As previously mentioned, they are attracted to pastors and church leaders who are defined by personal holiness. People have a deep desire for what is real and to listen to leaders who have spent time with God. I have come to believe your community will line up for churches whose pastors and leaders have lives fully devoted to Him.

John Maxwell teaches everything rises and falls on leadership. So what does leadership that rises and falls look like in a post-pandemic world for pastors and church leaders? See where you fit on the following list:

Pre-Pandemic Church Growth	vs.	Post-Pandemic Church Growth
Personal Preferences	vs.	Personal Holiness
What You Do	vs.	Who and Whose You Are
Bible as a Reference	vs.	Bible as Primary
Pastors Communicating	vs.	Pastors Delivering a Message
Prayer as a Task	vs.	Prayer as a Lifestyle
Skills	vs.	Sanctification
Opulence	vs.	Obedience
Being Led by Trends	vs.	Being Led by God's Word
Transaction	vs.	Transformation
Product	vs.	Process
Looks Like the World	vs.	Set Apart from the World
Competencies	vs.	Character

LEADER DEVELOPMENT VERSUS LEADERSHIP DEVELOPMENT

Leadership is all about character. In Minneapolis, Minnesota, is a landmark eatery called The 5–8 Club. Its specialty is a world-famous hamburger called the Juicy Lucy. For those unfamiliar with the Juicy Lucy, it is a hamburger with cheese on the inside of the patty rather than on top. This local cuisine has become so popular, it has been featured on the Travel Channel's *Man V. Food*. I have had the privilege of eating a Juicy Lucy, and it lives up to the hype!

The owners of this restaurant understand a significant leadership principle—It's what is on the inside that counts!

Leaders need to develop in two primary areas—Leadership development and leader development. Though the terms sound similar, there is a world of difference between the two.

- Leadership development is developing the skills, talents, and abilities to carry out a task or assignment given to you by God. This speaks to competencies. It is about doing.

- Leader development is becoming the type of man or woman capable of carrying out a task or assignment given to you by God. This speaks to character. It is about being. It is these the types of pastors, the ones focused on leader development, who are leading growing churches in a post-pandemic culture.

Too often, leaders focus more on leadership development (books, podcasts, conferences, training, networking, etc.) than leader development (prayer, Bible study, accountability). When this happens, a leader's skills, talents, and abilities can take them to a place where their character cannot sustain them.

So when a high-capacity leader has moral failure or a public fall from grace, I am rarely surprised. I immediately think they most likely put a heavier focus on their leadership development than their own leader development. Subsequently, their skills outpaced their character. The fall was inevitable.

For a leader to have the internal qualities needed to be mighty and continually move people from pandemic to progress, the following are what he/she needs to have on the inside:

1. Worldview—Is yours biblical?

2. Core Values—Are your guardrails clearly defined and nonnegotiable?

3. Standards—Are you living out your values?

4. Character—Does your private life reflect your public persona?

5. Integrity—Do you keep your word?

6. Honesty—Do you tell the truth?

7. Passion—Do you own the result?

8. Trustworthiness—Can people count on you?

9. Purity—Do your eyes look at the right things? Does your mind think on the right things?

10. Energy—Do you have a strong work ethic?

11. Intelligence—Are you a continual learner? Are you curious?

12. Focus—Do you avoid distractions and leverage your efforts and resources toward the right things?

13. Attitude—Is yours positive?

14. Humility—Can you say, "I'm sorry."

15. Emotional and Physical Endurance—Do you have what it takes to complete the journey?

16. Generosity—Are you unselfish?

17. Externally Focused—Do you see the intrinsic value of people and put others' interest ahead of your own? Are you kind, gentle, caring, and tender-hearted?

18. Health—Does your diet, rest, and exercise position you for long-term influence?

19. Finances—Do you tithe? Are you a saver or a slave to debt? Do you practice sound financial principles?

20. Self-Control—If you can't lead yourself, you can't lead others.

Finally, there have been countless leaders who were uniquely gifted but did not possess the necessary ingredients on the inside to sustain their success. However, don't be too quick to pass judgment on these individuals. There by the grace of God go you and I. We all possess the capacity to do likewise. Apart from Jesus Christ and the Holy Spirit's work in a person's life, it is impossible to achieve the twenty qualities listed above.

So in the future, if someone calls you a "Juicy Lucy Leader," take it as a compliment. They are impressed by what you have on the inside! Like many though, I could stand to lose about five-ten more pounds. on the outside. No Juicy Lucys for me!

ELITE PREACHERS

A mighty man of character who prioritizes leader development over leadership development is Pastor Nate Galloway. For six years I had the privilege of sitting under his leadership as the family pastor at Piedmont Church in Marietta, Georgia. If you don't know Nate, you should. He is a mighty man, an incredible husband and father, incredibly kind, and an elite preacher. In full disclosure, Nate is also one of my dearest friends and has endorsed this book.

In the fall of 2019, Nate was continuing our church's message series focused on the second chapter of the book of Ruth. The sermon dealt with how you go from having bitterness toward God (end of chapter 1) to being grateful because you have been blessed by God (end of chapter 2). His message was anointed, inspiring, challenging, comforting, and deeply impactful.

As I broke down the contents of his message, I gleaned the twenty-four practices of an elite preacher that you will read below. First is the practice followed by a supporting quote from Nate's message.

1. An elite preacher paints a picture of the Gospel. "Ruth is so amazing because it paints a picture of the Gospel for us."

2. An elite preacher teaches the Scriptures and sovereignty of God. "Two things we see from the book of Ruth. We see the sovereignty of God. God is the absolute authority and he is in complete control . . . Nothing happens apart from Him."

3. An elite preacher reminds us God is working in our lives. "Another theme we see is the providence of God. God begins to intervene and work in our lives."

4. An elite preacher puts things into proper perspective for us. As mentioned previously, John Piper wrote, "God is always doing 10,000 things in your life, and you may be aware of three of them."

5. An elite preacher wants what is best for us. "What every woman is looking for . . . 'You'll be safe here and we'll protect you.'"

6. An elite preacher helps us deal with life's toughest moments. "It's tough in the moment. Then we look back on our lives and see that God had not left us or forsaken us."

7. An elite preacher preaches in the name of God. "The name of God is mentioned twenty-three times in just eighty-five verses in the book of Ruth because God is working through the entire story."

8. An elite preacher wants us to have provision and blessing. "Always remember, no matter what is happening in your life, always come back to God. Always come back to His provision and blessing."

9. An elite preacher understands our struggles. "I understand the struggle of when the worst news, or season, or day of your life comes. I know the struggle to be mad at God . . . You don't want to run to God. You want to run away from Him. You don't want to pray to God. You want nothing to do with Him."

10. An elite preacher tells us about our sin. "When you keep Him at a distance, when you run from Him, when you're watching online and won't step into a church because you're mad at God, you and me are keeping everything we could possibly need in those difficult moments, we are keeping it away from our lives."

11. An elite preacher tells us where to find what we desperately need. "If you don't come back to Him, you'll never find what you desperately need."

12. An elite preacher tells us where to find forgiveness. "So come back home so God can move, so He can provide, so He can bless, so He can meet you right where you are."

13. An elite preacher pleads with us to come back to Jesus. "Every need that you have, every struggle you have, you have to come back to Him."

14. An elite preacher teaches us what is certain in life. "Always know God cares about you. God sees you. God does love you. And nothing can change that."

15. An elite preacher wants us to take our cares to God. "We can go to God with the things we care about because He cares about us."

16. An elite preacher reminds you and I how much God loves us. "God, help us to believe that no matter what's happening, that God, You are in control and You care and love us. You love me."

17. An elite preacher teaches God is working in our lives, even when we cannot see it. "Even when you can't see it, God is at work. He is working throughout all the unseen circumstances. He is in the 'it just so happened' moments of our lives."

18. An elite preacher brings peace and comfort. "He's not abandoned us. He sees you. He sees me. Come back to Him. He is working. He is intervening."

19. An elite preacher also personally struggles when things in their life are falling apart. "I do not have a problem with God's sovereignty and His providence when everything's good. I have a problem with it when everything's falling apart."

20. An elite preacher also struggles personally with God's sovereignty and providence. "I know what it's like to struggle with God's sovereignty and providence when a doctor looks at you and says, 'Your three-year-old has cancer.'"

21. An elite preacher always reminds us about what Jesus did on the cross. "Does anyone remember this moment right here? (a picture of Jesus hanging on the cross) That's not the end of the story. That's just the beginning. In three days, He's alive."

22. An elite preacher tells you and I how much God wants to save us. "When you ask, 'God, why don't you do something?' He says, 'I am. I'm saving the world. I'm saving you.'"

23. An elite preacher invites us to the cross. "I just to invite you to the cross, invite you to Jesus who understands."

24. An elite preacher prays for us and over us. "I want to pray for you and over you."

Once again, preachers are not communicators. Each week, they have a responsibility to deliver a specific message from God to a specific group of people to address the specific needs in their lives at a specific point and time in human history. Being a pastor is a high and holy calling.

PASTOR KEVIN LLOYD

A second mighty man is Kevin Lloyd. Kevin is an extraordinary ministry coach for CourageousPastors.com and executive pastor for LifePoint Church in Wilmington, North Carolina. There Kevin oversees a multi-campus team running several thousand each Sunday. Recently, I had the privilege of being in a session where he taught pastors and church leaders the value of "big days and growth engines." You will notice several of his thoughts line up with Pastor Benny Tate's on churches who grew in onsite attendance during the pandemic.

The most important thing a growing church must have is a growing leader. Kevin confirmed this with his opening comment, "Overflow begins with what God is doing inside of us." He also added, "We're guilty of incremental thinking, rather than exponential thinking." It was then Kevin unpacked a number of areas of focus churches must have to position themselves for exponential growth in their onsite audience.

"To have exponential growth and a big attendance day, you need focused urgency. You need to give people something outside of just Christmas and Easter. Pick a big day and invite your friends on that day. Work everything in the church toward that day. Put it on the calendar twelve-to-sixteen weeks out. Afterward, provide focused leadership. This is necessary for synergy. Work backward from that Big Day. As a leader, you have to stay focused.

"Then focus your ministries. Conduct a calendar audit of your church. You have to cancel things and pause things so you can look outward. Focus the messaging to your community. It needs to make sense on the community calendar. Make sure you speak to the pain points in your community. Make your serving strategic.

"You should also focus your teaching. Begin with an evangelistic sermon series, then a discipleship coaching series, followed by an evangelism training series. During this series, focus on your invites. Have one invite card sitting on each chair for several weeks leading up to the Big Day. For this to be successful, you must have focused prayer. Prayer is the foundation of any successful ministry initiative, especially large evangelistic efforts.

"And finally, focus your connections. A crowd doesn't make a church, but it can become one. The number one value for your follow-up is relationships. Your guests need to feel they are cared for. In follow-up texts, ask if a pastor can pray for them and schedule a tour of your church. As a special touch, also find out their favorite cup of coffee and have one waiting on them when they arrive."

Kevin concluded this incredible time of equipping by saying, "You need to elevate urgency (of the Big Day). And when you do that, some people will say it's too much. This separates good leaders from great leaders. Pressure crushes rocks and creates diamonds."

PASTOR MATTHEW CORNETT

Speaking of pressure, few professions have the enormity of pressure like that of being a senior pastor in a local church. In 2014, the Princeton Church of God located in Princeton, North Carolina, was a struggling congregation. The church had an average weekly attendance of 150 and was deeply divided. Intense conflict existed over music styles, chairs versus pews, and several other items. It was in this pressure-filled environment that God called Matthew Cornett to pastor.

What happened in the following eight years was truly a move of God. The church experienced 17 percent growth during the pandemic year of 2020, followed by 30 percent in 2021! The church now runs over 700 in average weekend attendance. Lives are being changed. Through a partnership with INJOY Stewardship Solutions, Princeton Church recently exceeded its campaign goal by $1.5 million! I sat down with Pastor Matthew to learn the best leadership practices needed to regain lost momentum and generate sustained church growth. What I gleaned from our time together were six habits of pastors who are mighty and lead growing churches.

First, pastors who are mighty and lead growing churches trust God. Pastor Matthew was not called to be a church planter. Rather, he was called to help resuscitate and revitalize a church. Pastor Matthew said, "Trust the Head, the Cornerstone of the Faith and what He is calling you to do." Pastors of today's growing churches know that obedience is more important than systems or the latest trends. He said, "Hear the voice of God and do whatever He tells you to do. And He'll honor that."

Second, pastors who are mighty and lead build unity. Pastor Matthew preached out of Numbers in his interview sermon. He fearlessly told the church, "The reason you are here is not because of your prior pastors. The reason you are here is because of you. It's time to repent, and it's time to turn to God." Instead of a negative vote for this pastoral candidate, the entire church went to the altar and repented after the message. Upon being voted in, Pastor Matthew continually reinforced what God told him was the church's core issue. "For a year, every message I preached had a thread of unity built into it." He stayed on message as God reconciled countless relationships.

Third, pastors who are mighty and lead growing churches develop a great staff. Pastor Matthew acknowledge, "My staff was the reason this was successful." They freed him up to do what he did best and what God had called him to be as the church's pastor.

Fourth, pastors who are mighty and lead own the result. You knew passion would come into play, didn't you! As the church's capital campaign began, a minimum goal was set at $1.5 million with a high goal of $2.2 million. But Pastor Matthew was trusting God for audacious things and wanted to exceed any bar set by INJOY Stewardship and their consultant Jeff Shortridge.

He decided to attend 10–20 percent more one-on-one dinners with high-capacity givers than was recommended. In addition, he went to dinners with everyone in the tier just below high-capacity. Pastor Matthew even went to one-on-one dinners with nongivers whom he thought had the potential to play a significant part in what God was doing at Princeton Church. Pastor Matthew was trusting God for great things, but he personally owned his role in the campaign's success.

Fifth, pastors who are mighty and lead growing churches disciple these high-capacity leaders. It is one thing to meet with high-capacity leaders. It is another thing completely to cast a compelling vision and call these individuals to sacrificial action. This is where Pastor Matthew excelled. Shortridge coached him through the structure and language of these times together. Pastor Matthew would ask his leaders, "What's your favorite part of the church? What do you love? Why do you come to the church?"

Sixth, pastors who are mighty and lead grow themselves. For these meetings to be their most effective, it required personal growth from Pastor Matthew himself. It required him to develop a new level of self-awareness. The advice he now gives pastors is, "Get over guilt. You're not raising money for you. All you're doing is asking people if they want to be a part of what God is doing. So get over yourself."

An additional benefit of these meetings was it strengthened the relationships between Pastor Matthew and the church's high-capacity leaders. The strengthening of these relationships also gave Pastor Matthew a unique insight into the minds of high-capacity leaders. He observed, "As pastors, we sometimes accuse leaders of being controlling when all they're really doing is leading. All they really want to do is be heard. They've never been afraid to give me their opinion, but they've also never been afraid to say, 'I'm not the CEO. You are.' Let them speak. Just because they disagree with you doesn't mean they're not going to back you."

The most valuable component of a capital campaign is the pastor's calendar and his or her willingness to meet with key leaders. The following was Pastor Matthew's advice:

- "Every pastor has different strengths. Use yours where God has strengthened you."
- "You've got to have very clear communication with your leadership that during this season of growth, I'm going to have to keep my focus primarily on two things—the thing that I'm great at, that one thing, and this campaign."

- "Guard our family time. Guard our personal time."
- "Pastor, if you're doing it by yourself, you're doing it wrong."

As previously mentioned, the campaign results were incredible. The church received commitments of $3.7 million! To God be the glory! This was $1.5 million above their goal.

CHRISTMAS

One final thought for pastors is on the subject of Christmas. I have become deeply concerned over the commercialization of Christmas, not just in the world, but specifically in the church.

Christmas is, and only is, about Christ! I'm afraid Christmas is becoming an optical illusion. Our eyes are being tricked into thinking what we see is what really is. All the lights, trees, Santas, treats, decorations, gifts, parties, shopping, and exhaustion is what Christmas has become for Christians. Satan wants us to have a holly, jolly Christmas, but he wants us to have it apart from Christ. Santa has become a graven image. As a result, Jesus hasn't been placed in the back seat of the bus. He's been left in the dust.

Christians are not to celebrate Christmas like the culture does. We are of another world. The question we must all answer, particularly as pastors and church leaders, is where is Jesus, His Word, His kingdom, and His great commission in our personal Christmas?

CLINT HURDLE

Personal holiness is obviously not limited just to pastors. I want to close this chapter on faith by talking about a person who embodies all the qualities discussed in this book—former National League Manager of the Year Clint Hurdle. When asked, during the online Zoom Bible study frequently mentioned, how you can delight in the Lord on the baseball field, this mighty man identified four specific areas. Though he was discussing the sport of baseball, what he shares applies to each of us regardless of where we are.

First, you can delight in the Lord in your struggles. Stuggle is necessary for strength. Experienced leaders know the value of facing challenging times head-on. Coach Hurdle said, "I can speak on a personal behalf. A couple of different times having rebuilds in couple of different organizations and knowing the pain, the anguish, the hard work, the criticism, the cynicism that you get along the way."

Second, you can delight in the Lord in your success. Success if the pay-off for staying diligent and faithful during times of struggle. It is the result of pressing into your challenges rather than shrinking from them. Coach Hurdle continued, "And then to land it, to actually land it. And see the euphoria, the jubilation, the happiness, now the buy-in, the bandwagons. It was empty and now it's full. People can't get on it's so full."

Third, you can delight in the Lord's overflow of the blessings in your life to others. With a sense of great satisfaction, Coach Hurdle noted, "That part of it makes you smile but the part that transcends that is when the you look at the employees. You look at season-ticket sellers. You look at people working the stands. You look at people, the cartilage of your organization, embracing that ride. People downtown, the vendors, the hotels, the restaurants, the joy that it brings to so many."

Finally, you can delight in the Lord's faithfulness in your life. Coach Hurdle concluded, "And to know the fact that you stayed steadfast with God's plan. You continued to serve and show up through the mud. You put your boots on. You walk through the mud. You dealt with the mess, knowing that whatever is going to happen, you're still going to walk with Jesus all the way through this, and it's going to end like He wanted it to end."

Coach Hurdle's list of four items is a wonderful way to close out this chapter. Mighty men and women who move others from pandemic to progress delight in the Lord during their struggles and successes. They delight in how He uses them to bless others, and finally, they delight in His faithfulness.

Do you?

CHAPTER 7 STUDY AND DISCUSSION QUESTIONS

Who is Jesus Christ to you?

_____

_____

_____

What victories have you had as a leader recently? Where and to whom did the credit go and why?

_____

_____

_____

What are your values and standards of behavior?

_____

_____

_____

How do you define character? Are you a person of character? What areas of your life do you need to work on to improve your character?

_____

_____

_____

What does Christmas mean to you and your family and why?

_____

_____

_____

Conclusion

By the mid-2000s, USA Basketball had fallen on hard times on the world stage. What had been considered a birthright of Americans to be champions in the sport was no longer assumptive. In fact, since 2000, losing had become an uncomfortable, commonplace trend.

In the 2002 FIBA World Championships, the United States shockingly finished in sixth place. During the tournament, the team lost to Argentina, Spain, and Yugoslavia. Assistant coach George Karl said in a post-game press conference following one of the team's losses, "Money, greed, and the NBA, is that having an effect on our competitive nature? Yeah, you can write that." The United States was no longer dominant.

In the 2004 Olympics in Greece, the team was blown out in the preliminary round by Puerto Rico 92–73. Rather than being known as "The Dream Team," this group was now being called "The Cream Team." They lost again in the semifinal game versus Argentina 89–81. Team USA was forced to settle for the bronze medal.

Now coached by Mike Krzyzewski, the team failed again in the 2006 FIBA World Championships in Japan. During the semifinal contest versus Greece, they were defeated by a score of 101–95. As Jason Kidd said in the Netflix documentary *The Redeem Team*, "The scare factor (of playing USA Basketball) was gone."

KOBE BRYANT

Enter Kobe Bryant. Writer Bill Plaschke said, "No one brought more baggage to Team USA than Kobe Bryant." There were concerns about his selfishness, being a good teammate, loyalty, and alleged personal indiscretions. But upon his 2007 arrival, everything changed.

Chris Bosh said, "He always had a very serious demeanor." Kobe did not force relationships. In fact, he had few if any friends at all. Carmelo Anthony said, "He was a loner. He was by himself. He didn't need anybody . . . He's comfortable with that." Plaschke said he even sat by himself in the first 2008 Team USA meeting.

But Kobe had a greater objective. He was all business and came to the team to help restore America's greatness in the game of basketball. He told Anthony, "I'm tired of watching y'all lose." Kobe said in a 2015 interview, "We want to show the world we are the best basketball playing country." Kobe did his part in making that happen by literally changing the culture of Team USA Basketball.

Very early in the team's first practice scrimmage, Kobe was diving head-first for loose balls over and over again. Mega-stars didn't do that, but the best player in the world at the time was setting the tone. Intensity was increased. Necessary confrontations began taking place. Greater energy and commitment were now required from anyone associated with the team. Bryant knew the team full of star players needed to focus on "the dirty work" and basics for the team to be successful. Coach K said, "He had to show the guys he was all in, and the way to do that was to play defense." He added, "We've never had a practice like this." This all happened because of the arrival of Kobe Bryant.

Carlos Boozer and Anthony also told a story of going out to a club one evening while training in Las Vegas. When they returned to the hotel at 5:30 a.m., they discovered Bryant had not gone out the night before. While they were returning to get some sleep before practice, Bryant was actually rising before dawn to go to the gym and work out prior to practice. Every player, from LeBron James to Dwyane Wade to every other superstar, knew Kobe Bryant's dedication was on a different level than theirs. By week's end, the entire team was now rising early and working out at 5:00 a.m.

Kobe brought this level of urgency to the court as well. After avenging the loss to Greece 92–69, next came the defending champion Spain. Spain was led by Bryant's Los Angeles Lakers teammate Pao Gasol. Bryant and Gasol were like brothers. But for this tournament, Bryant had a different set of teammates, and he would make that immediately known in an emphatic way.

Kobe told his teammates, "The first play of the game, I know what they are going to run" and he said in terms unprintable for this book that he was running through Gasol's chest. Sure enough, as Gasol set a screen for a teammate, Bryant ran through him in such a way that it violently knocked him to the ground.

Remembering that moment, Gasol said, "He ran through my chest to send a message, not just to me, but his teammates saying, 'Hey, this might be my brother. I play with him. We're close, but I don't care about anything else but winning.'" To which they did. The group of individuals known as The Redeem Team would bring the men's basketball gold medal back to the United States.

And it was Kobe Bryant to set the culture. While he may or may not have had the character trait of the faith of the Mighty Men, Kobe was a person who brought production, passion, resilience, teambuilding, contentment, and courage to Team USA.

Kobe brought the production through his scoring and defense. He exhibited passion by focusing solely on what was necessary to win the Gold Medal. His resilience was on full display by overcoming his personal shortcomings and reputation to blend in with the team. He did so at such a level, he became the most respected member of Team USA. Kobe was content with who he was and did not need compete with LeBron James for who had the most influence on the team. And finally, he had the courage to not only take big shots in important games, you would expect that, but to also personally change in the area of relationships. He became more open and took a risk by inviting others into his life.

The question for you as a leader is do you have similar traits? If not, get together with a group of like-minded individuals and go through this book and study questions at the end of each chapter.

Team USA was the beginning of the second chapter of Kobe's career. He would go on to become an iconic figure. With God's help, perhaps this book can be a new start for you as well. It is only through Him that you will become truly mighty and move from pandemic to progress.

WHO ARE THE LEADERS WORTH FOLLOWING?

In a post-pandemic world with many competing voices, it is often difficult to know which leaders to listen to and follow. The following are some items that will help you eliminate the imposters.

Leaders worth following will ask great things from you. You can trust them. If they tell you something will happen, it almost always does. They see the bigger picture and make you feel like you matter. Leaders worth following have great conviction. Whether you believe what they are saying or not, they believe it. They are never satisfied but are committed to continual improvement and personal growth.

The best leaders will invite you into something special. They are building a great team and want you to be a part of it. These individuals have high energy. Moss and dust are not gathering on them because they are constantly charging ahead. They bring out the best in you and give you the confidence that you can accomplish anything. Follow leaders who are proven and have sustained excellence.

Finally, leaders worth following always point you back to Jesus Christ and His Word. There is no higher calling a leader can have because it is ultimately the Lord who makes us mighty. Allow the following verses to be a guide and anchor for you as you take the journey from pandemic to progress.

> Now I know that the Lord saves his anointed; he will answer him from his holy heaven with the saving might of his right hand. Some trust in chariots and some in horses, but we trust in the name of the Lord our God. They collapse and fall, but we rise and stand upright.
>
> —Psalm 20:6–8 (ESV)

> Blessed is the man who walks not in the counsel of the wicked, nor stands in the way of sinners, nor sits in the seat of scoffers; but his delight is in the law of the Lord, and on his law he meditates day and night. He is like a tree planted by streams of water that yields its fruit in its season, and its leaf does not wither. In all that he does, he prospers. The wicked are not so, but are like chaff that the wind drives away.
>
> —Psalm 1:1–4 (ESV)

> Delight yourself in the Lord, and he will give you the desires of your heart.
>
> —Psalm 37:4

Only be strong and very courageous, being careful to do according to all the law that Moses my servant commanded you. Do not turn from it to the right hand or to the left, that you may have good success[a] wherever you go. This Book of the Law shall not depart from your mouth, but you shall meditate on it day and night, so that you may be careful to do according to all that is written in it. For then you will make your way prosperous, and then you will have good success.

—Joshua 1:7–8 (ESV)

Keep the charge of the Lord your God, walking in his ways and keeping his statutes, his commandments, his rules, and his testimonies, as it is written in the Law of Moses, that you may prosper in all that you do and wherever you turn.

—I Kings 2:3 (ESV)

For what will it profit a man if he gains the whole world and forfeits his soul? Or what shall a man give in return for his soul?

—Matthew 16:26 (ESV)

Commit your work to the Lord, and your plans will be established.

—Proverbs 16:3 (ESV)

Fear not, for I am with you; be not dismayed, for I am your God; I will strengthen you, I will help you, I will uphold you with my righteous right hand.

—Isaiah 41:10 (ESV)

You shall remember the Lord your God, for it is he who gives you power to get wealth, that he may confirm his covenant that he swore to your fathers, as it is this day.

—Deuteronomy 8:18 (ESV)

My son, do not forget my teaching, but let your heart keep my commandments, for length of days and years of life and peace they will add to you. Let not steadfast love and faithfulness forsake you; bind them around your neck; write them on the tablet of your heart. So you will find favor and good success in the sight of God and man.
—Proverbs 3:1–4 (ESV)

And the Lord brought about a great victory that day
—2 Samuel 23:10 (ESV)

Bibliography

INTRODUCTION

Charles R. Swindoll, *David: A Story of Passion & Destiny*, W Publishing Group, a Division of Thomas Nelson, Inc., 1997, 60–70.

CHAPTER 1–PRODUCTION

Tom Mullins quote was from training session with INJOY Stewardship Solutions, August 3, 2022

Ryan Hawk, *The Pursuit Of Excellence: The Uncommon Behaviors Of The World's Most Productive Achievers*, 2022, McGraw Hill, 2022, 155-157

Jiro Dreams of Sushi, Sundial Pictures, 2012

L. Jon Wertheim, *Strokes Of Genius: Federer, Nadal, and the Greatest Match Ever Played*, Mariner Books, 2010, 114-116

Exploring hamstrings with Jurdan Mendiguchia, the world's most in-demand physio, February 5, 2022, Marca.com, https://www.marca.com/en/football/spanish-football/2022/02/05/61fee-15ae2704eb79e8b457d.html

Carolyn Dewar, Scott Keller, and Vikram Malhotra, *CEO Excellence: The Six Mindsets That Distinguish the Best Leaders From The Rest*, Scribner, 2022, 69-70

Pol Ballus and Lu Martin, *Pep's City: The Making Of A Superteam*, BackPage and Polaris, 2022, 5

Joe Banner and Ben Elsner, The Resurrection Of Chiefs Kingdom: What's Changed in Kansas City, December 12, 2021, https://www.the33rdteam.com/the-resurrection-of-chiefs-kingdom-whats-changed-in-kansas-city/, https://www.the33rdteam.com/

CHAPTER 2—PASSION

Noah Smith, *The Washington Post*, May 24, 2022, "Surfing a record 86-foot wave took guts. Measuring it took 18 months." https://www.washingtonpost.com/sports/olympics/2022/05/24/surfing-record-sebastian-steudtner/?utm_campaign=mb&utm_medium=newsletter&utm_source=morning_brew

Marcus Thompson II, *The Athletic*, May 23, 2022, "Andrew Wiggins punctuates his status as a certified Warriors core member," https://theathletic.com/3328262/2022/05/23/andrew-wiggins-warriors-dunk-highlights/

BBC News, "Eight-year-old's handwritten novel takes Idaho town by storm," February 2, 2022, https://www.bbc.com/news/world-us-canada-60229749?utm_campaign=mb&utm_medium=newsletter&utm_source=morning_brew

Reach The People Media, Deion Sanders Teaching The Importance Of SACRIFICE, October 19, 2022, https://www.youtube.com/watch?v=o0pbdZggxfs&t=359s

The Athletic, "Chris Paul's 30 points propel the Suns past Pelicans in Game 1 win: 'He's built for these moments,'" April 18, 2022, https://theathletic.com/news/chris-paul-suns-win/MzGcK6ziYfrI/?source=dailyemail&campaign=601983

Sydney Isenberg, "Colorado Springs man makes history after pushing peanut with his nose to Pikes Peak summit," https://www.thedenverchannel.com/news/local-news/colorado-springs-man-makes-history-after-pushing-peanut-with-his-nose-to-pikes-peak-summit?utm_campaign=mb&utm_medium=newsletter&utm_source=morning_brew

CHAPTER 3–RESILIENCE

Crawford W. Loritts, Jr., *Leadership as an Identity: The Four Traits of Those Who Wield Lasting Leadership,* Moody Publishing, 2009, 40.

Carey Lohrenz, *Fearless Leadership: High-Performance Lessons from the Flight Deck,* 2014 Alke Publishing, 223.

Chris Power, January 22, 2021, https://247sports.com/player/stetson-bennett-iv-89844/, ‹No Cheating, No Whining. Stand Up in the Rain›, December 24, 2022, https://www.thedaily.coach/p/youre-missing-boat,

Kaneptune, July 14, 2020, "Why 11 Babies Have Been Born In Antartica", https://medium.com/good-to-know/why-11-babies-have-been-born-in-antarctica-7409e0cc98f

Nicola Smith, January 20, 2022, "Tongan 'Aquaman' Survives tsunami and 27 hours at sea," https://www.telegraph.co.uk/world-news/2022/01/20/tongan-hailed-aquaman-surviving-tsunami-27-hours-sea/

https://twitter.com/DukeWBB/status/1544291475608899584

Per https://mindsetmadebetter.com/2022/06/success-is-not-final-failure-is-not-fatal-it-is-the-courage-to-continue-that-counts/, Winston Churchill's quote comes from his 1946 commencement speech at the University of Miami

"If you want to win big, you have to be ready to lose big.", May 22, 2022, https://twitter.com/SkySportsPL/status/1528467191565373440?ref_src=twsrc%5Etfw%7Ctwcamp%5Etweetembed%7Ctwterm%5E1528467191565373440%7Ctwgr%5E578be-4f28063985b7868dbb6597ef882477ad5fe%7Ctwcon%5Es1_&ref_url=https%3A%2F%2Fbriandoddonleadership.com%2F2022%2F05%2F29%2F7-lessons-on-how-leaders-should-handle-defeat%2F

John Piper, *God Is Always Doing 10,000 Things In Your Life*, January 1, 2013, https://www.desiringgod.org/articles/god-is-always-doing-10000-things-in-your-life

Chris Low, ESPN.com August 25, 2022, "Nick Saban on coaching through the end of his contract in 2030: 'I feel like a young man,'" https://www.espn.com/college-football/story/_/id/34460192/nick-saban-coaching-end-contract-2030-feel-young-man

CHAPTER 4—TEAMWORK

Ted Nguyen, *The Athletic,* October 6, 2022, "Why this San Francisco 49ers defense has potential to be historically great," https://theathletic.com/3655415/2022/10/06/san-francisco-49ers-defense-demeco-ryans/

"Coach Lou Holtz added, 'I've coached teams with good players and I've coached teams with bad players. I'm a better coach when I have good players!'", *Talent Is Never Enough: No Matthew How Gifted You Are, These 13 Choices Will Make You Better*, John C. Maxwell, Thomas Nelson, Inc., 2

Allison Finch, June 25, 2022, Record-breaking python discovered in Florida Everglades, https://www.accuweather.com/en/weather-news/record-breaking-python-discovered-in-florida-everglades/1207619?utm_source=twitter&utm_campaign=accuweather&utm_medium=social, AccuWeather.com

Kendra Andrews, ESPN.com, June 14, 2022, "Andrew Wiggins' huge double-double effort in Game 5 puts Golden State Warriors on verge of another NBA title," https://www.espn.com/nba/story/_/id/34088217/andrew-wiggins-huge-double-double-effort-game-5-puts-golden-state-warriors-verge-another-nba-title

Billy Graham once said, "A coach will impact more people in one year than the average person will in an entire lifetime." https://www.azquotes.com/quote/825836

The Conversation.com, August 19, 2022, "Sandcastle engineering—a geotechnical engineer explains how water, air and sand create solid structures, https://theconversation.com/sandcastle-engineering-a-geotechnical-engineer-explains-how-water-air-and-sand-create-solid-structures-188208?utm_source=-join1440&utm_medium=email&utm_placement=newsletter

ESPN.com, May 23, 2022, "Why Mbappe chose PSG over Real Madrid: The critical moments that led to his decision," https://www.espn.com/soccer/paris-saint-germain—frapsg/story/4673162/why-mbappe-chose-psg-over-real-madrid-the-critical-moments-that-led-to-his-decision

Peyton Manning's Summer School, NFL Films, 2016

CHAPTER 5—CONTENTMENT

April 6, 2022, The Daily Coach, "How Bill Self Contextualized Adversity," https://thedailycoach.substack.com/p/self-contextualizing-adversity?s=r

James Pearce, *The Athletic,* May 4, 2022, "Half-time highlights were non-existent—Klopp's words turned Liverpool from vulnerable to impregnable," https://theathletic.com/3292594/2022/05/04/half-time-highlights-were-non-existent-klopps-words-turned-liverpool-from-vulnerable-to-impregnable/

https://www.morningbrew.com/daily

Alan Stein Jr. with Jon Sterneld, *Sustain Your Game: High Performance Keys to Manage Stress, Avoid Stagnation, and Beat Burnout,* Hachette Go, 2022, 8, 19.

John Talty, *The Leadership Secrets of Nick Saban: How Alabama's Coach Became the Greatest Ever,* John Talty, Matt Holt, 2022, 84.

CHAPTER 6—COURAGE

"I think this is the first time in ukranian history that we have a truly ukrainian president" a former advisor to the Ukrainian president, @ErinMcLaughlin, February 28, 2022, https://twitter.com/ErinNBCNews/status/1498286046123118596?s=20&t=ObvzN-8rOZC3ZkbLRocpFFw

Jamiel Lynch, Dakin Andone, and Pete Muntean, CNN.com, May 11, 2022, "A passenger with no flying experience landed a plane at a Florida airport after the pilot became incapacitated," https://www.cnn.com/travel/article/florida-passenger-lands-plane/index.html

AP News, July 20, 2022, "Man saves 5 from house fire; jumps out window to save girl," https://apnews.com/article/fires-indiana-lafayette-ebac06275f72a4604bf8f102e7a768d9?utm_source=-join1440&utm_medium=email&utm_placement=newsletter

Noah Smith, May 24, 2022, Surfing a record 86-foot wave took guts. Measuring it took 18 months. https://www.washingtonpost.com/sports/olympics/2022/05/24/surfing-record-sebastian-steudtner/?utm_campaign=mb&utm_medium=newsletter&utm_source=morning_brew, The Washington Post

The City of Texarkana Facebook Post, December 29, 2021

TonyRobbins.com, "How To Avoid Relationship Arguments," https://www.tonyrobbins.com/ultimate-relationship-guide/how-to-avoid-arguments-relationship/

CHAPTER 7—FAITH

Ronnie Gomez, NeonOne.com, September 15, 2021, "10 Year-End Giving Statistics Every Fundraiser Should Know," https://neonone.com/resources/blog/year-end-giving-statistics/

Be sure to check out Brian's First Book
2021: THE YEAR IN LEADERSHIP

Do you feel ill-equipped to handle the leadership challenges of a pandemic and post-pandemic world? If so, you no longer have to.

In 2021, author, speaker, consultant, and podcaster Brian Dodd helped equip countless leaders across world through his content. Over 80 of his most popular articles make up the pages of 2021- The Year In Leadership: The Stories of Faith, Athletics, Business, and Life Which Inspired Us All.

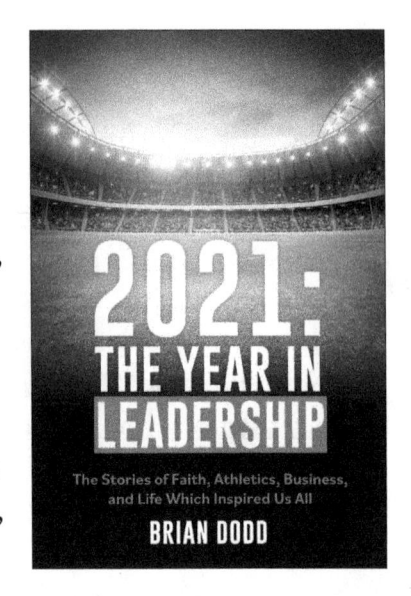

Each chapter is filled with wisdom and insights from the leaders who succeeded and struggled during 2021. Brian takes these lessons from all walks of life and gives you practical steps on how to best use them in your own leadership. As you will discover, the stories are entertaining, challenging, inspiring, and sometimes even sobering.

The best leaders are the ones who sense and seize opportunity in the midst of chaos. Brian thinks this describes you. This is why this book was written. By learning the lessons from 2021, it helps ensure you have the potential to become the leader God meant for you to be in 2022.

"I have had the privilege of calling Brian Dodd a friend for almost 25 years. One thing has proven true through all of those years and that is Brian Dodd always leaves me better than when he found me. Whether it is his amazing blog, incredible books or just a lunch to pick his brain, Brian will always take good and make it better! His ability to glean insights from everyday life & even athletics and apply leadership principles to them is incredibly unique! Who wins……we all do! If you open this book and read, I promise you will be better too!"

Mike Linch
Senior Pastor NorthStar Church
Host of the Linch with a Leader Podcast